# Def....ing
# Genocide

# DEBATES IN WORLD HISTORY

**Series Editor:** Peter N. Stearns, George Mason University, USA

**Editorial Board:** Marc Jason Gilbert (Hawaii Pacific University, USA), Heather Streets-Salter (Northeastern University, USA), Sadiah Qureshi (University of Birmingham, UK)

Bloomsbury's *Debates in World History* series presents students with accessible primers to the key debates in the field of world history, from classic debates, such as the great divergence, through to cutting-edge current developments. These are short, argumentative texts that will encourage undergraduate-level history students to engage in the practice of doing history.

**Published:**
*Debating the Industrial Revolution*, Peter N. Stearns
*Debating Modern Revolution*, Jack R. Censer

# Debating Genocide

## LISA PINE

BLOOMSBURY ACADEMIC
LONDON • NEW YORK • OXFORD • NEW DELHI • SYDNEY

BLOOMSBURY ACADEMIC
Bloomsbury Publishing Plc
50 Bedford Square, London, WC1B 3DP, UK
1385 Broadway, New York, NY 10018, USA

BLOOMSBURY, BLOOMSBURY ACADEMIC and the Diana logo are trademarks
of Bloomsbury Publishing Plc

First published in Great Britain 2019
Reprinted 2020

A catalogue record for this book is available from the British Library.

A catalog record for this book is available from the Library of Congress.

ISBN:  HB:      978-1-3500-3543-0
       PB:      978-1-3500-3542-3
       ePDF:    978-1-3500-3544-7
       eBook:   978-1-3500-3545-4

Series: Debates in World History

Typeset by RefineCatch Limited, Bungay, Suffolk
Printed and bound in Great Britain

To find out more about our authors and books visit www.bloomsbury.com
and sign up for our newsletters.

*For Gaby and Sasha*

# Contents

# List of Figures

# List of Maps

# Preface

I have been teaching a course on genocide to final year undergraduate students at London South Bank University since 2006. When I first started teaching it, the field of genocide studies was comparatively new and quite small. In the last decade or so, the field has grown exponentially and the subject is also much more widely taught in universities. I had not come across a short, introductory book to accompany my course and when the new series 'Debates in World History' came to my attention, I suggested to the history editors at Bloomsbury that a book on genocide might fit the series and discussed a proposal for this book with them. My editor, Rhodri Mogford, and the series editor, Peter Stearns, both thought it was worth taking forward and I am very pleased to have had their support for this title from the start. The field of genocide studies is now very large, complex and still growing fast. If this book succeeds in helping students to navigate it and to engage with this challenging and difficult subject in a meaningful way, then it will have been a worthwhile project for me as an author and as an educator.

I would like to thank my students over the years that have taken my course, for participating in interesting (and, of course, sometimes difficult) discussions and debates in our seminars, especially the cohort of 2016–17, when I was preparing the manuscript. I would also like to thank the Scouloudi Foundation in association with the Institute of Historical Research for the grant of a publication award. Together with the publisher, I would like to express my thanks to Getty Images for permission to reproduce all the illustrations inside the book, as well as the cover image. I am grateful to the staff at the Wiener Library in London for their help with my research. I am thankful to all the friends and colleagues who have been willing to discuss ideas and offer advice, including Dan Stone, who read and commented on the book proposal for me, and Dan Michman and Catherine Baker for sharing their expertise with me. I am grateful to the anonymous proposal reviewers for their positive responses, helpful comments and constructive advice. I would like to thank my brother-in-law, Michael Fields, for kindly offering to read the draft manuscript. My thanks are especially due to Marius Turda and Alex Alvarez, who took valuable time away from their own work to read the whole manuscript for me and to offer their suggestions for improvement. I would like to thank Rebecca Jinks and Benjamin Lieberman too, for their careful reading of the manuscript, which helped me to improve the text. I would like to express my gratitude to my research assistants, Rebecca O'Neill, Adam Newman, Sasha Skovron, Meena Mehdi and Lauren Cudmore, for their hard work and enthusiasm. I am thankful to my editor, Rhodri Mogford, for all his help and patience throughout the publishing process. It has made a huge difference to have the continuity of working with the same editor on three consecutive books over the last few years. I would also like to express my gratitude to his colleagues at Bloomsbury in editorial, production and marketing for their efforts on my behalf, and to my copy editor, Juliet Gardner, for her hard work and efficiency. My thanks are also due to Merv Honeywod and James Tupper for all their hard work turning the manuscript into this book. I would like to thank my family for their encouragement and forbearance whilst I was writing this book – it has not been easy to live with this subject. I am thankful to my wonderful husband, Andy, who is always supportive of my writing projects, endures their process with tremendous good grace and is always my first reader. Finally, I would like to thank my two lovely daughters, Gaby and Sasha, who have listened patiently throughout as this project progressed from initial idea to completion. I dedicate this book to them.

Lisa Pine
London, 2018

# Introduction:

# The Concept of Genocide and its Definition

**W**hy study genocide? Why debate and discuss this challenging and difficult subject? There are a number of compelling reasons. Firstly, genocide is a crucial subject in global history. Not just in Europe, but right across the world, genocides have tainted human history and need to be understood. Secondly, it is not only history that we seek to comprehend, but in exploring the field of genocide studies, we touch a range of other subjects across the social sciences and humanities including, but not limited to, sociology, anthropology, psychology and political science. We encounter a whole host of complex and often vexed academic debates. Thirdly, it is important to treat this subject because of our concern for humanity and our sense of justice and morality. Genocide is associated with the darkest aspects of human nature. By studying it, we try to understand how and why people have engaged in atrocities, and what this says about the human condition. Fourthly, we hope that our studies may make a difference. In getting to grips with this subject, we can consider how to prevent genocide in the future. Finally, our study changes us, and the way we view humanity as well. Studying genocide obliges us to confront difficult, distressing and uncomfortable issues. It is emotionally challenging, as well as academically engaging. A critical study of this subject can help us to comprehend and respond to many important aspects of our contemporary political and social life – including power, agency, conflict, human rights and responsibilities – and to gain compassion, wisdom and maybe even the inspiration to make a difference in the world, through our quest for understanding. For all these reasons, the study of genocide is significant.

An essential starting point for an analysis of the subject of genocide is a definition of the term itself. Sociologist Leo Kuper stated: 'The word is new, the concept is ancient.'[1] Indeed, the roots of genocide may be traced back from prehistory and antiquity through into the modern and contemporary eras. The phenomenon of genocide was, as Winston Churchill noted, 'a crime without a name'. In seeking to define genocide, it is useful to begin with Raphael Lemkin (1900–59), a Polish-Jewish jurist, who first coined the term genocide as 'the destruction of a nation or an ethnic group'.[2] He believed that each and every nation had a purpose and a cultural contribution to make to humanity: 'The diversity of nations, religious groups and races is essential to civilisation, because every one of these groups has a mission to fulfil and a contribution to make in terms of culture.' Lemkin defended the group rights of peoples against extermination, but also, as he later put it in 1946, against the 'crippling' of a people as well, not simply mass murder.

Lemkin used the term genocide to encompass a global and long-standing historical phenomenon. Genocide is a neologism that puts together the Greek word *genos* (race or tribe) with the suffix *cide* from the Latin word *caedere* (to kill). Lemkin defined a new norm and was a major protagonist in bringing about specific prescriptions for a change of behaviour in international relations. His campaign originated with his perception of a significant omission in international law before the Second World War. State sovereignty meant that individual states were at liberty to inflict violence upon members of their own populations, as other states would not intervene. Lemkin's work led to the drafting of the United Nations Convention against genocide. In the aftermath of the Second World War, as the true horror of Nazi rule was revealed, the legitimacy of state sovereignty came into question. Lemkin campaigned tirelessly to bring about his norm against genocide, one that has now partly (though not entirely) displaced that of state sovereignty in these matters.

Lemkin's chief concern was with ethnic and national groups. He was not primarily interested in cases in which political groups were the targets of destruction, because he was concerned with the devastation of ethnic groups and their cultures, which could not be resuscitated once destroyed. Lemkin emphasised that mass killing was only one part of the phenomenon of genocide, although clearly a very important part. He defined genocide as 'the destruction of a nation or an ethnic group', but added:

Genocide does not necessarily mean the immediate destruction of a nation, except when accomplished by mass killings of all members of a nation. It is intended rather to signify a coordinated plan of different actions aiming at the destruction of essential foundations of the life of national groups, with the aim of annihilating the groups themselves. The objectives of such a plan would be disintegration of the political and social institutions of culture, language, national feelings, religion, and the economic existence of national groups, and the destruction of the personal security, liberty, health, dignity, and even the lives of the individuals belonging to such groups. Genocide is directed against the national group as an entity, and the actions involved are directed against individuals, not in their individual capacity, but as members of the national group.[3]

In 1948, a legal definition of genocide came into being, with the promulgation of the United Nations Convention on the Prevention and Punishment of the Crime of Genocide.[4] This defined genocide as: 'Acts committed with intent to destroy, in whole or in part, a national, ethnical, racial or religious group, as such.' According to the UN Convention, genocidal acts encompassed not only 'killing members of the group', but also 'causing serious bodily or mental harm to members of the group', 'deliberately inflicting on the group conditions of life calculated to bring about its physical destruction in whole or in part', 'imposing measures intended to prevent births within the group' and 'forcibly transferring children of the group to another group'. Again, this definition is much broader than mass murder. In both Lemkin's definition and that of the UN Convention, mass murder is just one aspect of genocidal policy. Both Lemkin and the UN Convention stress the obliteration of a group, 'as such', not necessarily the physical liquidation of its members.

What are the key features or characteristics of genocide? The conceptualisation of Gregory Stanton, Founding President of Genocide Watch, presents a useful starting point in this regard. He initially described genocide as a process that moves through 'eight stages'. These are: classification, symbolisation, dehumanisation, organisation, polarisation, preparation, extermination and denial. The first stage, classification, is characterised by the distinction of people into different groups. This is a categorisation of 'them and us', based upon race, religion, nationality or ethnicity. The second stage, symbolisation, entails the naming of groups as 'other' and distinguishing them or marking them out from the rest of society. Symbols are often forced upon 'enemy' groups, such as the Yellow Star worn by European Jews under Nazi rule. The third stage is dehumanisation or the denial of the humanity of the target group. Its members are vilified as vermin, pests, diseases or even inanimate objects. The fourth stage is organisation. Genocide is always intentional, planned and orchestrated from above, often executed by military personnel or specially trained militias. Polarisation is the fifth stage of the genocide process. Groups in society are separated, for example, by the banning of marriage or social interaction. The enemy group is alienated and isolated. The sixth stage is preparation. This involves the physical separation of members of the enemy group and/or their forced deportation. This segregation, confinement or deportation to or from a particular area is a significant moment. The term 'ethnic cleansing' has been applied to this process. The seventh stage of the genocide process is mass killing or destruction of the group. The eighth and final stage in the process of genocide is denial. The perpetrators deny their crimes and try to hide the evidence.

More recently, Stanton has incorporated two more stages into his initial framework, creating a ten-stage model as follows: classification, symbolisation, discrimination (the use of legal methods, or political power, to deny the rights of a targeted group), dehumanisation, organisation, polarisation, preparation, persecution (identification and separation on grounds of religion or ethnicity), extermination and denial. However, it is significant to note that whilst this is a useful model, it is not intended to present the process of genocide as linear. It is important to understand that some stages may take place

– have applied a breadth of scope to the discourse of genocide studies. This cross- and multi-disciplinary approach has led to the creation of a very vibrant and distinctive field of genocide studies. Comparative research has become increasingly popular over recent years and there have been a number of significant changes in the study of the subject. The Holocaust has come to be seen as a heuristic device to illuminate the processes of other genocides. It has been contextualised within broader processes of nation-building and empire-building over a longer period of time. The mass killings in Rwanda and the former Yugoslavia in the 1990s necessitated a new approach to the study of modern genocide. There is no longer a need for establishing moral superiority and credentials, or for competitive hierarchies. It is more significant now for scholars to make points of comparison in a non-competitive way and to seek out similarities as well as differences between cases of genocide, in order to try to understand it and to prevent its recurrence. David Moshman has presented a useful and convincing argument, stating that: 'Given that every genocide is unique, any prototype-based concept of genocide will distort one's understanding of some genocides as it filters them through whatever genocide is taken as central and defining.'[11] Christian Gerlach's concept of 'extremely violent societies' and Benjamin Valentino's argument that the important question is not whether a case of mass violence counts as genocide or not, but how we explain episodes of mass violence whatever their motivation, are salient too.[12] In addition, part of the interpretative problem is that genocide is 'more a legal term than a historical one', as historian Donald Bloxham has argued.[13] He further explains that genocide is 'a classic example of the past examined teleologically: a retrospective projection'.[14] Furthermore, recent research has explored new areas, such as the relationship between economics and genocide, and the relationship between genocide and civil war.[15] Debates on the social psychology of perpetrators, as well as considerations of the perspectives of victims and bystanders, are also significant.[16] In a recent book, political scientist Michael Jasinski argues the case for 'delving into the relationship between leaders and followers'.[17] He applies social movement and leadership theories to illuminate leader–follower interaction and its place in genocide. Sociologist Damien Short has examined the relationship between genocide, ecocide (deliberate destruction of the environment) and colonial settlement, shifting the paradigm of genocide studies. He argues that much of the field of genocide studies 'has failed to appreciate the importance of culture and social death to the concept of genocide' and offers an analysis of 'ecocide as a method of genocide'.[18] He contends that it is impossible to understand genocide fully 'without a strong appreciation of a range of environmental factors and ecological issues such as anthropogenic climate change, land use and abuse, soil degradation, water contamination and shortages, biodiversity loss and habitat destruction'.[19] Alex Alvarez also maintains that the challenges and changing circumstances brought about by environmental factors 'will heighten the risk for the development of communal and ethnic violence, war, and genocide'.[20] Historical examples show us that environmental and climactic factors can result in societal or state collapse, conflict and large-scale violence. Alvarez suggests that 'climate change will facilitate the development of various structural, ideological, and psychological conditions that escalate the risk of large-scale organized violence'.[21]

The controversies surrounding definitions of genocide, as well as the myriad scholarly perspectives and themes posed by the subject, inform the nature of this book. In addition, whilst the motives and actions of perpetrators often and rightly take up considerable scholarly attention, the perspective of victims is, of course, also highly significant in our understanding of genocide. To this end, short extracts from survivor accounts and testimonies are included throughout the book, in order to illustrate the nature of victims' experiences and to give the victims of genocide their voice. It is worth noting here too that estimates of death tolls can vary quite considerably depending on the source one reads, and these numbers can be highly contested. In this book, the figures used are those most widely agreed upon by experts in the field as accepted numbers or what seem to be reasonable estimates where we simply do not know actual death tolls for a variety of reasons.

# Outline

This book is intended as a concise introduction to a complex field with a large and fast-growing scholarly literature. It presents an accessible point of entry into the subject, introducing major debates and the current state of research. Readers and students may extend and deepen their knowledge through the sources indicated in the further reading at chapter ends. It is impossible in a book of this length to do more than choose a number of significant case study examples to illustrate the nature of genocide. These have been selected because they are largely regarded as paradigmatic cases and ones that students are most likely to encounter in their courses. This book aims to help the reader to gain a sense of how genocide developed in specific, significant case study examples. It has been difficult to select which cases to include and which to omit. There have been so many different episodes of mass murder and genocide across the globe that it is not possible to treat them all here. The omission from this book of, among others, the genocides in Indonesia and East Timor, Bangladesh, Burundi, Guatemala, Iraq and Ethiopia does not lessen their significance.

Chapter 1 of this book treats the subject of colonial genocides. The impact of European colonisation on peoples across the globe is sometimes described or defined as genocide. To be sure, there are significant links between colonialism and genocide. In particular, the depopulations especially of North and South American Native Indian populations and Aboriginal populations in Australia have been some of the most momentous in history. However, if genocide signifies a deliberate intention to eradicate a group of people, then these depopulations were not necessarily or definitively genocides. European colonisation certainly had a profound effect on indigenous populations of colonised territories, but was there in all cases the intention to destroy the group? This issue has divided experts. This chapter examines the links between colonialism and genocide. It begins with an examination of the European first contact with the New World and its implications for the native populations in North America, as well as Australia. It then moves on to consider the impact of more modern imperial expansion, in particular at the end of the nineteenth century and the start of the twentieth century. It treats the colonial rule of Belgium in the Congo, as well as that of Germany in German South West Africa (Namibia). On the continent of Africa, the often-overlooked genocide of the Herero in Namibia was the first genocide of the twentieth century. The case of the Herero shows very clearly that the degradation and dehumanisation of a people led to atrocities and genocidal acts against them. German officials and settlers in German South West Africa regarded the Herero and Nama peoples as subhuman and inferior. The extermination of the Herero on these grounds also gave justification to the perpetrators of the genocide; it was considered acceptable and even necessary to kill the Herero on the grounds of their racial inferiority.

Chapter 2 examines the Armenian genocide undertaken by the Young Turk regime or Committee of Union and Progress (CUP) during the First World War. Until comparatively recently, this was also a much-neglected genocide. In this case, we see the impact of an exclusivist ideology upon the victim group. The Armenians did not fit into the 'new order' envisaged by the Young Turks, and hence they were massacred and annihilated. The ardently nationalist Young Turk movement came to abandon multinational 'Ottomanism' and to replace it with exclusive 'Turkism'. It targeted the Armenians because of their linguistic, cultural and religious differences, believing that they had no place in Turkish society. The Armenian genocide perpetrated by the Turkish government in 1915 resulted in the death of an estimated 1 million civilians. Contemporary observers described the violence towards the Armenians as 'a massacre like none other' and 'a massacre that changes the meaning of the word massacre'. This chapter analyses the causes and key characteristics of the Armenian genocide, and examines the main historiographical debates pertaining to the subject.

In Chapters 3 and 4, we turn to the Nazi regime. Chapter 3 examines the history of the Holocaust or the *Shoah* ('catastrophe'). The Holocaust or the 'Final Solution' was the Nazis' attempt to wipe out European Jewry during the course of the Second World War. Largely through the use of mobile killing squads in the eastern arena of the war and death camps in Poland, some 6 million Jews perished at the hands of the Nazis and their collaborators. The scale and the process of the mass killings were unprecedented. The death camp at Auschwitz has endured as the most powerful symbol of the Holocaust. This chapter analyses the steps leading up to the Holocaust as well as examining its main characteristics. The chapter takes into account the most up-to-date scholarship on the Holocaust. Among other salient issues, it highlights recent research on the opportunities that pillaging

Jewish property presented for the Nazis, for ordinary Germans and for others. Being able to raid and plunder strengthened support for the regime. Encouraging local populations to pillage Jewish property in this way brought them into complicity with the regime and its persecution and genocide. This chapter analyses the key historiographical debates and recent advances in Holocaust research.

Chapter 4 examines the history of the Nazi genocide of the Sinti and Roma, known as the *Porrajmos* ('devouring'). The 'Gypsies' (Sinti and Roma) remained forgotten victims of National Socialism for many decades. The Nazi perpetration of the genocide of the European 'Gypsy' population was not widely recognised until the 1980s. This chapter evaluates the evolution of Nazi policies towards the Sinti and Roma throughout the 1930s – discrimination, exclusion, segregation, sterilisation and medical experimentation – culminating in the *Porrajmos* during the war. The chapter also examines the relationship between the 'Gypsies' and German society. The German people's long-standing distrust and dislike of the 'Gypsies' made it easier for the Nazi regime to implement its policies against them. The majority of the population took little interest in the plight of the 'Gypsies'. Many were pleased that as undesirables, the 'Gypsies' were kept away from them. They viewed the persecution of the 'Gypsies' as a justified struggle against an antisocial and criminal element that did not fit into German society. There was virtually no empathy or compassion among the German people towards 'Gypsy' victims of Nazi policy. This sentiment was also replicated right across East–Central Europe, which made it much easier for the Nazi regime and its collaborators to carry out genocidal policies against the Roma in these areas. This chapter also analyses the reasons for which this genocide was long forgotten and not well studied or researched until comparatively recently.

Chapter 5 moves to a discussion of Cambodia under the Pol Pot regime between 1975 and 1979. It explores whether the massacres that took place under the Khmer Rouge can be more accurately described as genocide or politicide, or both. It explains the ideology of this communist regime, and the power and paranoia of its leader. Pol Pot's Khmer Rouge regime perpetrated mass killings against specifically targeted sections of the Cambodian population, including Buddhists and other religious and ethnic minorities. The Cambodian case is particularly interesting. The massacre of ethnic and religious groups by the Khmer Rouge leadership in Cambodia can be termed genocide. This chapter explains how not all scholars concur on this point. The Khmer Rouge regime, led by Pol Pot, instigated wholesale massacres of its people. These mass murders, which took the lives of one-quarter of the Cambodian population, were partly politically motivated, but certainly they were partly genocidal as well.

Moving to a critical decade in the history of genocide, the 1990s, Chapter 6 examines genocidal violence in the former Yugoslavia, in particular in Bosnia-Herzegovina and Kosovo. Yugoslavia began to break up as Slovenia and then Croatia declared their independence in 1991. Serbia, the most powerful of the six Yugoslavian republics, had its own ambitions to achieve a 'greater Serbia' and was determined to prevent the secessions. Between 1991 and 1999, during the course of its break-up into separate states, the former Yugoslavian federation saw widespread atrocities and ethnic cleansing perpetrated by all sides in a multi-sided conflict, involving Serbians, Croatians and Bosnians. The slow and passive responses from the international community acted as a green light for Serbia, in particular, to continue its ethnic cleansing campaign in order to achieve its nationalist aims. This chapter analyses these events and their outcome, as well as recent debates around the subject.

Chapter 7 focuses on the genocide in Rwanda. In April 1994, Rwanda witnessed the unleashing of the genocide of the Tutsi by the ruling Hutu-led government. The genocide was the culmination of the construction of differences and enmity between the Hutu and the Tutsi, which had begun in the colonial era and became exacerbated during a civil war between 1990 and 1994. The wife and closest advisers of President Habyarimana were directly responsible for planning the genocide. The *interahamwe* ('those who stand together') militias were in charge of the killings on the ground. They mobilised the majority of the Hutu to kill the Tutsi. Indeed, the scale of popular participation in the mass slaughter was one of the most extraordinary features of the Rwandan genocide. This genocide claimed some 800,000 lives. It was met with international indifference and inaction. This chapter examines the causes and key characteristics of the Rwandan genocide, in addition to academic discourse and debate in relation to this event.

Whilst genocide is very much a phenomenon associated with the twentieth century, we can see clearly that not only did episodes of genocidal violence predate the twentieth century, but also they have continued into the twenty-first century. Chapter 8 examines the Darfur genocide in Sudan, where the first genocide of the twenty-first century unfolded in a conflict that began in 2003. This arose from a long-standing struggle over land, between Arab pastoralists and settled African agriculturalists. The tensions between them had intensified as a result of drought and increasing desertification of the land. Arab pastoralists moved southwards from the arid, northern part of Darfur, into territories occupied by the Fur, Massalit and Zaghawa tribes. A series of violent clashes was exacerbated by the Khartoum government, which sided with the Arab pastoralists, supplying them with arms. In response, the Sudan Liberation Army (SLA), a rebel group, launched its own insurgency for the failure of the government to offer protection to these groups against Arab raiders. Khartoum responded with a savage campaign of ethnic cleansing that was intended to drive out the peoples of this region and to replace them with Arab settlers. The Sudanese government was responsible for the perpetration of atrocities against the local populations in Darfur. Arab militias, known as *Janjaweed* (men on horseback), terrorised the peoples of this region. Their actions were characterised by burning, rape, pillage and the mass murder of entire communities. This chapter considers the causes, key features and consequences of this genocide.

Chapter 9 treats a number of significant themes and selected issues that go beyond the individual case studies. In particular, it highlights four key areas of analysis and debate: genocide and gender; genocide prevention; genocide and justice; and memory and memorialisation. This does not mean that other aspects are unimportant; it simply reflects the nature of a short book and the need for a decision on what to include and what to omit. This chapter begins with a consideration of the theme of gender. Gender-based distinctions provide an important analytical tool in the discussion of genocide. Initially, there was some scepticism about the employment of gender as a lens for the study of genocide, with arguments suggesting that it trivialised the crime. However, by now gender has become an established aspect of study within the field of genocide studies. This section is followed by a discussion of the debates around the prediction and the prevention of genocide, and analyses the R2P (Responsibility to Protect) initiative. The next part of the chapter deals with the subject of justice, examining some key examples of international justice including the Nuremberg Tribunal and the International Criminal Tribunal for the Former Yugoslavia (ICTY) and the International Criminal Tribunal for Rwanda (ICTR). Finally, the chapter moves on to examine the issues of memory and memorialisation, which have been much debated.

The concluding chapter sums up the overall content of the book, reflecting on key issues and debates, as well as suggesting questions for further discussion and study. A greater knowledge and comprehension of the concept of genocide and its execution, as well as its implications, is significant to our perception of society and of humanity. We live in a world where violent societies and mass murder continue to exist. Genocide is not an unplanned, uncalculated phenomenon. It is instigated and carried out with deliberation, calculation and planning. It is not a random act. Education, knowledge and understanding may be a step in the direction of its prevention.

## Questions for Further Discussion

1 What is genocide?

2 Why does genocide occur? What are the preconditions and what are the triggers?

3 Who are the perpetrators and what are their motives?

4 What are their justifications for their actions and their crimes?

5 Who are the victims?

## Further Reading

Anderton, C. and Brauer, J. (eds), *Economic Aspects of Genocides, Other Mass Atrocities, and Their Prevention* (Oxford, 2016).
Bloxham, D. and Moses, Dirk A. (eds), *The Oxford Handbook of Genocide Studies* (Oxford, 2010).

Gellately, R. and Kiernan, B. (eds), *The Specter of Genocide: Mass Murder in Historical Perspective* (Cambridge, 2003).

Gerlach, C., *Extremely Violent Societies: Mass Violence in the Twentieth Century World* (Cambridge, 2010).

Jones, A. (ed.), *New Directions in Genocide Research* (Oxford and New York, 2012).

Jones, A., *Genocide: A Comprehensive Introduction* (Oxford and New York, 2017).

Kiernan, B., *Blood and Soil: A World History of Genocide and Extermination from Sparta to Darfur* (New Haven, CT and London, 2007).

Levene, M., *Genocide in the Age of the Nation State, Volumes 1 and 2* (London, 2005).

Levene, M., *The Crisis of Genocide Volume I, Devastation: The European Rimlands 1912–1938* (Oxford, 2014).

Levene, M., *The Crisis of Genocide Volume II, Annihilation: The European Rimlands 1939–1953* (Oxford, 2014).

Mann, M., *The Dark Side of Democracy: Explaining Ethnic Cleansing* (Cambridge, 2005).

Meierhenrich, J., *Genocide: A Reader* (Oxford, 2014).

Midlarsky, M., *The Killing Trap: Genocide in the Twentieth Century* (Cambridge, 2005).

Spencer, P., *Genocide since 1945* (Oxford and New York, 2012).

Stone, D. (ed.), *The Historiography of Genocide* (Basingstoke, 2010).

Valentino, B., *Final Solutions: Mass Killing and Genocide in the Twentieth Century* (Ithaca, NY, 2004).

# 1

# Colonial Genocides

Colonialism, a type of imperialism, engendered the establishment of rule and subordination by a state or power over another people or peoples. Settler colonialism entailed the imperial power sending new settlers to a particular territory or land. Intrinsic to its nature was the occupation or taking over of land for settlement. The resultant displacement and routing of existing peoples from such lands was sometimes linked to genocide against indigenous populations. Imperialism and colonialism were processes that marginalised the status of the original inhabitants. Indigenous peoples were thus transformed from dominance within a territory to subordination, and even removal. This was largely because the settlers had a sense that the indigenous peoples should somehow 'fade away' or 'disappear' in the face of their advance. More brutal tactics often occurred when local populations resisted the newcomers and failed to 'melt away' or 'vanish'. In these circumstances of confrontation on the frontiers, more extreme 'solutions' sometimes occurred. In some cases, entire tribes were wiped out through violence, for example, in North America and Australia. The European colonialism that took place at the end of the nineteenth century was motivated by a number of significant factors. Political aims included the acquisition of overseas territory to enhance national glory and status. Economic motives included the desire for new areas for capital investment, as well as the acquisition of raw materials and new trading opportunities. In addition, imperialism was underpinned by a sense of superiority among the governing nations, such as Britain, France and Germany, over the colonised peoples in the lands they came to rule. This sentiment, in turn, arose from racial and Social Darwinist theories that permeated European intellectual life during the last decades of the nineteenth century.[1] This had an impact on how European colonisers regarded and behaved towards the native peoples in the lands they acquired.

Both colonialism and genocide are significant historical processes, occurring across the globe and across centuries, but the connections between these two processes are not so straightforward to establish in all cases. Did colonialism lead to genocide?[2] This question has created considerable debate among experts. Elazar Barkan states: 'Mutilation and death of indigenous peoples were almost a continuous component of imperialism and colonialism over the centuries.'[3] Ward Churchill and David Stannard have written controversial works about the genocide of Native American populations in the USA.[4] Stannard states that inadvertent deaths, for example, through disease, were going on at the same time as purposeful genocide. He claims that the two were somehow intertwined and interdependent. George Tinker argues that even if intentions were relatively benign – perhaps as in the case of missionary activity – then the consequences were significant. Tinker states that missionaries actively participated in the 'cultural genocide' of Native Americans. He contends that the missionaries were guilty of 'complicity in the destruction of Indian cultures and tribal social structures – complicity in the destruction . . . and in the death of the people to whom they preached'.[5] Damien Short has argued that 'when indigenous peoples, who have a physical, cultural and spiritual connection to their land, are forcibly dispossessed and estranged from their lands they invariably experience "social death" and thus genocide'.[6] There is also a polarised debate on the question of genocide in Australia. Many commentators argue that there were genocidal policies against Aboriginal populations.[7] Other scholars reject this. Whilst they do not deny that large numbers of Aborigines perished, they absolve the colonial and national governments of responsibility for this, and deny that the European colonisation of Australia was genocidal. In addition, there have been heated debates in the context of settler policies in Australia about the forced removal of indigenous children from their families.[8]

Colonialism necessarily entailed a power relationship between the settlers and those living in conquered lands. Colonial conflicts were underpinned by an ideology that considered indigenous populations to be 'barbaric' and 'inferior'.[9] In this chapter, a small number of cases have been selected to demonstrate the complexity of this debate and to underline the care needed in the discussion of colonialism and genocide. This chapter takes examples from the Americas, the Congo Free State, German South West Africa and Australia to illustrate the links between colonialism and genocide.

# North America

The history of colonial settlement of the North American continent is complex and contested. Before the arrival of Europeans in the sixteenth century, settled communities of Native Americans with their own origin stories were engaged in intensive hunting, fishing and plant cultivation. There has been a wide range of estimates of the numbers of Native Americans who died as a result of European settlement in the New World – most experts today concur that the death toll was 4–5 million. To be sure, there was a very drastic decline in Native American numbers after 'first contact' with the Europeans. However, it is necessary to consider how and why this decline occurred. Care needs to be taken with the attachment of the term 'genocide', which signifies deliberate intent to destroy a group. In the case of the Native Americans and the policies of the European settlers, intention to deliberately wipe out whole peoples was not always evident. The most significant cause of depopulation among Native American peoples was the introduction of 'Old World' diseases to the 'New World', in particular cholera, smallpox, scarlet fever and typhoid, to which the indigenous populations had no immunity. In addition to the spread of contagious diseases, there were a number of other factors that impacted upon the numbers of Native American peoples. These were warfare with Europeans as well as murderous acts committed by Europeans; intertribal warfare; forced relocation; the introduction of alcohol, which sometimes had a devastating effect on native populations; and the destruction of food supplies, especially buffalo. The number of buffalo fell from an estimated 60 million before European settlement to 1 million in 1875 and fewer than 1,000 in 1895. This had a profound and devastating impact on the way of life and capacity to survive of native populations. From the 1860s, the building of railways across the USA led to the near-extinction of the buffalo. This was devastating for the American Plains societies, who were nomadic and followed the seasonal movements of the buffalo herds, as an important source of food, clothing and shelter. It completely destroyed their traditional way of life.

Whilst first encounters with Europeans brought devastating depopulations through disease, further catastrophe for the native peoples was engendered by the competition between the Spanish, British and French settlers for dominance. By the beginning of the nineteenth century, the Cherokees, Chickasaws, Choctaws, Creeks and Seminoles had reached a successful accommodation with American society. However, the Indian Reservation Act of 1830 forcibly removed these tribes and their land was given over to cultivation. American policies of population removal to reservations and dispossession of lands was far reaching. These tribes were forced to move to territories that lay hundreds of miles across the continent. The Choctaws were transferred westwards between 1831 and 1834. Alex Alvarez has noted that at least one-quarter of them died before they reached the new Indian territory in Oklahoma.[10] A similar proportion of Cherokees died between 1838 and 1839 on their journey, which was known as the Trail of Tears (see Map 1).

Benjamin Madley has written about California's Yana Indians as a case of genocide in the USA.[11] Before 1847, there were between 2,000 and 3,000 Yana Indians living in an area of California between the Sacramento River and the Southern Cascades of Northern California. Their number declined to 1,800 in 1852 and to just twenty in 1880. What was the cause of this depopulation? The California gold rush brought 9,000 newcomers to this part of California between 1848 and 1850. They engaged in violent conflict with the indigenous populations. The Yana had three choices, none of which were ideal: they could live among the newcomers and serve them in different ways, with no legal rights; they could fight them, but their bows and arrows were no match for the rifles of the newcomers; or, they could retreat into the mountains. The Yana people were compelled to move higher and higher into the mountains where the possibilities for life became increasingly difficult to sustain, with very cold temperatures, snow and little food. Between 1850 and 1858, new immigrants destroyed the food sources of the Yana and then in 1858 articulated a

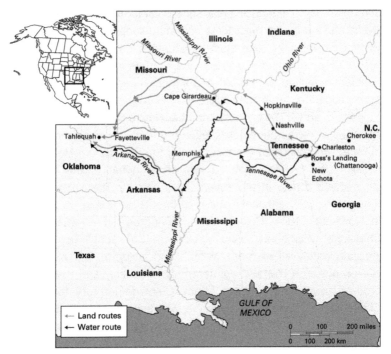

**MAP 1** *'Trail of Tears'.*

new goal – to remove the Yana by any means, including extermination. Massacres had become increasingly frequent throughout the 1850s and state-sanctioned capturing and killing operations began in 1859. Between 1860 and 1871, volunteer death squads hunted down the Yana and killed them. The local press in 1862 reported that 'the only way to deal with those rascals is to shoot them on sight' and 'companies should be raised to hunt down . . . and punish them and that punishment should be extermination'. Hence, a policy that had started out as retaliation against the Yana for taking food stocks from settlers escalated to state-sanctioned mass killing and culminated in the aim of total extermination. Madley has also examined the history of the Tolowa people of northwest California and southwest Oregon. He shows how their population declined from approximately 5,000 in 1851 to 900 in 1856.[12] Whilst he notes that the spread of European diseases partly explained this catastrophic population decline, he also demonstrates that genocide was another factor that contributed to it. He carefully portrays massacres and state-supported killings of the Tolowa Indians. His case study encourages us to 're-evaluate the accepted emphasis on disease and warfare in Native American population decline' and to arrive at a more 'nuanced understanding' of this aspect of American history.[13]

Hence, settler policy towards the Native Americans included episodes of deliberate extermination throughout a significant period of time, exemplified by the massacre of the Pequots (an Algonquian-speaking tribe who inhabited territory in what is the state of Connecticut today) in the seventeenth century. There were many other cases of intentional massacres throughout the next centuries. In November 1864, Colonel John Chivington led an attack on a Cheyenne Village at Sand Creek in Colorado. His soldiers indiscriminately killed men, women and children. This massacre, carried out by a military regiment, was expressly and deliberately ordered by the government of the Colorado Territory to kill the Cheyenne. This particular massacre was part of a larger genocidal campaign against the Cheyenne and the Arapaho communities with the intention of destroying them. There were deliberate massacres carried out across the North American continent, in which many indigenous communities were completely, or almost completely, annihilated. For example, the genocide of the Yuki in California in the mid-nineteenth century involved deliberate murder on the part of settlers and intentional colonial policy directed towards the demise of the Yuki. At the Battle of Wounded Knee, South Dakota, on 29 December 1890, 146 Sioux men, women and children were killed. General William Sherman, Commanding General of the US Army, believed that 'the only good Indian is a dead Indian'. This sentiment was not his alone. L. Frank Baum, author of The Wizard of Oz, claimed after the Battle of Wounded Knee: 'The best safety of the frontier settlements will be secured by the total annihilation of the few remaining Indians. Why not annihilation? Their glory has fled, their spirit broken.' Hence, massacre at the frontiers did occur. Benjamin Madley has convincingly argued that it is necessary to study genocide in North America on a case-by-case or nation-by-nation basis, in order to create a scholarly precision in our use of this contentious term.[14]

European settlement had a significant impact on the First Nations in Canada too. These communities faced a similar experience to the Native Americans in the USA, with massive depopulations among many of them. Most notable was the total destruction of the Beothuks of Newfoundland. Up to 2,000 Beothuks lived there at the time of first contact with European newcomers in the sixteenth century. By 1823, 96 per cent of them had perished. A combination of factors led to this demise – including a lack of availability of food sources, disease and outright murder by settlers. Legislation regarding Canada's First Nations was passed during the nineteenth century, defining their status, encouraging assimilation and removing children to Residential Schools.[15] The treatment of its First Nation inhabitants has been the subject of much scholarly debate and public enquiry in Canada. It has been contended that Canadian governments deliberately starved the native populations in order to make way for land-hungry European settlers. It has been argued further that there were also attempts to culturally assimilate the First Nations and thus destroy their identity and practices. This was indeed the case to a large extent. Whilst it is not possible to maintain that Canadian governments took part in wholesale mass murder and genocide, the arrival of European settlers certainly resulted in the displacement or destruction of Canadian First Nation communities.

## The Congo Free State

The devastation and suffering perpetrated in the Congo under Belgian colonial rule was brutal and horrific, described by Neal Ascherson as one of the 'most appalling slaughters' to have been engendered by human agency, but not always receiving prominent attention in the genocide literature.[16] Accounts from eyewitnesses, writers and scholars depict the brutality with which King Leopold II of Belgium ran the Congo Free State as his personal fiefdom, a Crown Domain, between 1885 and 1908. His administration of the Congo in this manner was an exception in the history of European colonialism. In the cases of all the other European colonies, the government of the colonial powers at least theoretically administered them. Leopold ruled the Congo as his own property. He ran it through the *Force*

*Publique*, a Belgian administrative cadre, and an African army of some 19,000 troops. This native army, controlled by Leopold's administration, carried out the genocidal aspects of Belgian rule in the Congo. Joseph Conrad's *Heart of Darkness* (1902), which described, through the words of the leading character, Marlow, the exploitation in the Congo, has become the iconic literary work on the subject. The 'heart of darkness' alluded to the Congo River, the imperial project, as well as human nature and the evil of which it is capable. Leopold's chief concerns in the Congo were the collection of ivory and rubber for export. In order to amass a large supply of rubber, he established a reign of terror and brutality in the Congo. The brutal *corvée* (forced labour) established by King Leopold in the Congo meant that rubber tappers and porters were exploited to the point of death through overwork and hunger, as vast areas were turned into forced labour camps for the production of rubber for export. Bloodshed was commonplace. Edmund Morel, a clerk of the Liverpool Shipping Company, first brought the exploitation to popular notice in a well-publicised campaign against the 'Congo atrocities'. His works on the subject included *King Leopold's Rule in Africa* (1904) and *Red Rubber* (1907). In 1904, he established the Congo Reform Association, an international protest group. Among its most notable members were Joseph Conrad and Arthur Conan Doyle. In 1908, King Leopold was forced by international pressure to give up his rule of the Congo. He sold it to the Belgian government and its administration was reformed.

Adam Hochschild has estimated that the population of the territory was 'reduced by half' under Belgian rule, from 20 million to 10 million people.[17] Eric Weitz concurs that 'the death toll ran into the millions'.[18] In certain cases, outright mass murder was the major cause of death. For example, Simon Roi, a Belgian state officer, bragged in 1899 about the killing squads that he commanded. However, Hochschild points out that outright murders were less significant than 'starvation, exhaustion and exposure' as causes of death. There was, furthermore, a recurring epidemic of sleeping sickness that claimed vast numbers of victims. The outbreak of sleeping sickness in 1901 alone killed 500,000 Congolese. Hence, there were a number of different factors that accounted for this great loss of life, including mass murder, starvation, exhaustion, exposure and disease. Most of the factors were a direct result of the policies of Leopold's 'extractive regime'.[19]

As Neal Ascherson has stated: 'The responsibility for this disaster is no less Leopold's because it was a compound one.'[20]

# German South West Africa

Germany, a latecomer in the course of the European imperialism of the nineteenth century, was determined to take its share of African colonies – among them, German East Africa and German South West Africa (see Map 2). Between 1883 and 1885, Germany annexed the territory of German South West Africa, now Namibia. There were four indigenous tribes living on this land: the Herero, the Berg Damara, the Ovambos and the Nama (also referred to as Hottentots). The Herero were cattle herdsmen, whilst the other peoples were nomadic hunter-gatherers. At first, German South West Africa attracted few

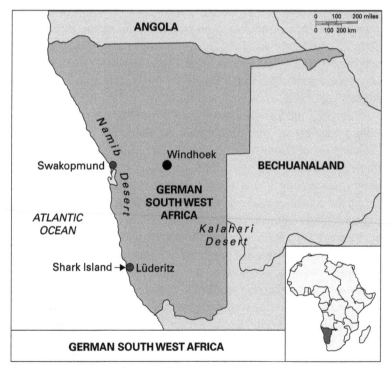

**MAP 2** *German South West Africa.*

German settlers and the governor, Major Theodor Leutwein, was able
to effect compliance without the need for arms. But at the turn of the
twentieth century, German farmers made the journey there and
railways were built. The Herero tried to maintain their way of life,
which centred upon their cattle. However, imperial rule was harsh
and the local tribes were increasingly forced off their land. Their cattle
were threatened and this engendered considerable bitterness among
the Herero. By the end of 1903, German settlers and farmers had
taken over 3.5 million hectares of land, out of 13 million hectares. This
pace of progressive loss of their land impinged considerably upon the
capacity of the Herero to preserve their traditions. In addition, many
Herero owed money to white traders. Leutwein issued an ordinance
on debt collection in the summer of 1903, which went into effect on
1 November 1903, and German traders began to call in their loans
swiftly in response to it. This caused much dissatisfaction among the
Herero. Furthermore, as increasing numbers of German settlers
came into the colony, they tended to regard the native populations as
a source of cheap labour or even to question whether it might be
better to eradicate them. They looked down on the Heroro, held them
in contempt and regarded them as animals, labelling them 'baboons'.
The Herero responded to the treatment they received from German
settlers with force.

In January 1904, the Herero chief, Samuel Maharero, instigated a
Herero rebellion against the German colonisers, hoping to drive the
Germans out of South West Africa.[21] They attacked German garrisons,
transport systems and farms. The Nama joined the Herero in their
efforts to stand up to the settlers. Nearly 150 Germans were killed
during the course of this uprising. The Herero used a surprise attack to
their advantage. Leutwein described the uprising as 'nerve-shattering',
but despite their initial success, in August 1904, the Herero were
surrounded and defeated at the Battle of Waterberg. The Herero rising
triggered a massive retaliation on the part of the German government,
which sent General Lothar von Trotha to the region. Von Trotha was a
hardened career soldier who had previously suppressed uprisings in
German East Africa. He stated: 'I know enough tribes in Africa. They
all have the same mentality insofar as they yield only to force . . . I
shall destroy the rebellious tribes by shedding rivers of blood and
money.' He was true to his word. His soldiers brutally massacred large

numbers · of Herero and Nama, and drove thousands into the inhospitable desert regions, where they met their deaths. As they fled the Germans followed them, killing men, women and children. Furthermore, the German troops patrolled the water holes, driving away or killing any Herero who tried to obtain water. On 2 October 1904, von Trotha made his *Vernichtungsbefehl* (annihilation order):

Within the German boundaries, every Herero, whether found armed or unarmed, with or without cattle, will be shot. I shall not accept any more women and children, I shall drive them back to their people – otherwise I shall order shots to be fired at them. This is my decision for the Herero people.

This destruction of the Herero was the decision of von Trotha, not the official policy of the German government. Indeed, there were protests about this policy in Germany, including within the German government, yet Jon Bridgman and Leslie Worley state that 'this was genocide because it was an attempt by representatives of the German government to destroy a whole people with the knowledge and the tacit approval of the Kaiser and the General Staff'.[22] The brutal conflict lasted four years and involved 17,000 German soldiers (2,000 of whom were killed). Isabel Hull has contended that the role of the military and its worldview was highly significant in this genocide. She argues that the atrocities committed against the Herero and Nama were so commonplace that they should be regarded as 'standard operating procedures'.[23] The German colonising power had the technological and administrative capacity to kill large numbers of people, who were regarded as an 'inferior' enemy. Hull maintains that the 'final solution' in German South West Africa developed out of military practices and that for von Trotha, a complete victory over the Herero was a military goal.

In addition, the Herero were rounded up and placed into internment or 'concentration camps', where they undertook forced labour and perished in large numbers. One such camp was located at Shark Island, another at Swakopmund – these camps were certainly striking forebears of the Nazi concentration camp system. There was a clear connection between the genocide of the Second Reich and that of the Third Reich in this regard. Shark Island inmates were utilised as a compulsory labour force in the railway construction of German South West Africa. Conditions at Shark Island were notoriously appalling and the prisoners there died of disease, overexertion in manual labour with insufficient nutrition, exhaustion, as well as violence and brutality. In addition, medical experiments were carried out in these camps on victims.[24] Herero women also suffered sexual exploitation and violence. The Herero were degraded, dehumanised and ultimately annihilated (see Figure 1).

By September 1905, there were very few free Herero left. Some 15,000 Herero (comprising men, women and children) were imprisoned in these camps. Approximately half of them perished as a result of forced labour and mistreatment. By the time the Germans left South West Africa, the Herero and the Nama had been decimated as peoples. It is estimated that out of some 80,000 Herero, only 15,000 remained. Of the 20,000 Nama, more than half had been killed. Those that remained lost their social and cultural identity, and had been reduced to a permanent state of forced labour for the German colonisers. This destruction of the Herero and the Nama bore the hallmarks of genocide. Scholars including Isabel Hull, Benjamin Madley and Jürgen Zimmerer have highlighted connections between

**FIGURE 1** *Execution of Herero in German South West Africa, circa 1907.*

German colonial policies in South West Africa and Nazi policies in 'the East'. Apart from the use of camps, transfer of knowledge was a significant factor with personnel working first in the German colonies of the Second Reich and later in the Third Reich.[25] Hull convincingly argues that 'Germany's imperial experience' laid 'solid foundations' for National Socialism.[26] Jeremy Sarkin concludes that Germany's extermination of the Herero was a 'calculated campaign' and that this 'intentional policy was nothing short of genocide'.[27]

# Australia

When Captain James Cook arrived in Botany Bay, in 1770, his discovery of the great southern continent was a momentous occasion for Britain. However, it was not considered a discovery by the indigenous populations, as they already lived there. Yet they were the victims of vast depopulations and in some cases of genocide.[28] The main reasons for the decline in the Aboriginal population included disease, malnutrition, the introduction of alcohol, decreasing birth rates, increased intertribal warfare and massacres. At first, the intentions of the settlers were relatively benign. The first governor of the colony in Sydney, Arthur Phillip, was instructed from London to 'conciliate' the affections of the Aborigines, live in kindness with them and punish those who tried to harm them. The initial intention of the colonial power was to civilise and Christianise the native inhabitants. The British Governor of Adelaide stated in 1835: 'Black men. We wish to make you happy. But you cannot be happy unless you imitate white men. Build huts . . . wear clothes.' The settlers saw no proper utilisation of the land by the Aborigines who were hunter-gatherers. However, the Aborigines were not interested in the settlers' pastoralism. In terms of land use, the viewpoint of the Aboriginal hunter-gatherers was completely at odds with the pastoralism of the newcomers. The concept of *Terra nullius* emerged – the land had no original inhabitants in a legal sense, and therefore the settlers believed they had legal and utilitarian justifications for their actions. They simply took the land as Crown Land, without negotiating at all with the Aborigines. As time went on, the settlers seized more and more territory for extensive pastoralism. Sheep grazing interfered with the traditional way of life of the Aboriginal populations. Between 1832 and 1850, 200,000 immigrants arrived in Australia. This led to increased competition for land. The settlers' desire for land led to confrontations between them and the Aboriginal populations. Violence erupted in frontier clashes between the newcomers and the native inhabitants, and in the absence of troops, the settlers took matters into their own hands as land hunger prevailed. Settlers took territory as they saw fit, with no concern for the interests of the Aborigines. This meant they blocked access to water and food sources, for example, in the Hawkesbury River area (New South Wales). Due to the immense size of the continent, whatever official colonial policy might have been, it took a very long time for it to be transmitted from metropolitan centres such as Sydney and even more so from London. Hatred and contempt came to characterise the settlers' attitudes towards the Aborigines, as the latter refused to be proselytised or to follow the white man's ways.

The destruction of the Aboriginal way of life appeared to be unavoidable with the arrival of increasing numbers of settlers in to Australia, seeking both land and gold. Dirk Moses argues that 'the colonization process undeniably had . . . a "genocidal effect" on Aborigines'.[29] Whilst the unintended effects of colonialism engendered most of the drastic depopulation, the assumptions and actions of European settlement contributed to the mass death of Aboriginal peoples too. At times, when Aborigines resisted the newcomers, as Dirk Moses has shown, policy makers were prepared to consider 'final solutions' to the 'Aboriginal problem'. Hence, the process of the colonisation of Australia changed over time; it had genocidal possibilities that could, but did not always, come into being. In many parts of Australia, colonialism occurred without genocidal measures. However, in specific places and at particular times, the newcomers became agents of genocide against the native inhabitants of the territories they settled. The Appin Massacre (1816) and the massacre at Warrigal Creek (1843) exemplified such violent atrocities. These processes and events bear striking similarities to those on the North American continent, discussed earlier in this chapter.

In Van Diemen's Land (now Tasmania), as the settler population increased from 2,000 in 1817 to 23,000 in 1830, a frontier war –

known as the Black War – escalated during the 1820s between the newcomers and the original inhabitants of the island, the Pallawah.[30] By 1830, 1 million sheep were being grazed in territory previously used by Aboriginal hunter-gatherers, which led the latter to attack settlers. Edward Curr, who ran the Van Diemen's Land Company, called for 'a war of extermination' against the Aborigines. Governor George Arthur attempted conciliation, but the new settlers pressurised and obliged him to take increasingly radical measures to protect them from the Aborigines. His efforts to sedentarise the Aborigines failed and were replaced by a reserve system, removing Aborigines from newcomers' lands. However, hostilities persisted, and in 1830, Arthur resorted to military action to remove Aborigines from settlers' territories. By this time, only a few hundred Aborigines had survived the conflicts with the settlers. Eventually, the settlers gave them the choice of moving to smaller islands off the coast of Tasmania or being shot. This amounted to a policy of forcible expulsion. About 200 Aborigines were moved to Flinders Island where attempts were made to civilise them – by 1838, only eighty remained alive. This policy remains a hotly contested issue among Australian scholars, with strong arguments made on both sides of the case.[31] Ann Curthoys contends that seeking 'to take the land whatever the consequences' is a 'genocidal process'.[32] Patrick Wolfe also shows that contests for land are often 'contests for life'.[33]

In Queensland, between the 1850s and the 1890s, a war of extermination against Aboriginal peoples occurred and the Native Police actively hunted down and killed Aborigines. In 1859, Queensland achieved independence from New South Wales and here the government directly represented the interests of the colonists, without intervention from Sydney or London. Queensland had an Aboriginal population of about 100,000. Frontier conflicts resulted in an average of fifteen to twenty settlers being killed each year, with a high of forty-six in 1874, during the northern gold rush. The government here used the Native Police – composed of Aborigines, not white settlers – to deal with the frontier crisis. The Native Police units were paramilitary forces that shot Aboriginal groups on sight. They had been used elsewhere in the 1830s and 1840s to prevent confrontations between settlers and Aborigines. In Queensland, the pastoralist settlers sought the relationship of power that they had and about their intentions towards them. The newcomers were in some cases at first paternalistic, relatively benevolent or benign, sometimes with the intention of Christian missionary activity as a motive. However, over time, relationships between the native populations and the settlers became increasingly tense. The motivations of the settlers became more self-seeking – land hunger and gold rush, for example – and their treatment of the original inhabitants became increasingly brutal. Colonisation processes certainly had socially destructive effects. When the settlers met resistance or unexpected responses, this led to increasing clashes of interests between themselves and the native populations of the lands to which they had come. The settlers hoped that the native populations would simply 'fade away' or 'vanish'. Settler colonialism resulted in the removal or destruction of pre-existing indigenous populations. However, there were huge variations in the history of colonialism across the globe and across several centuries.

The problem with applying the UN definition of genocide to colonial cases of mass death is that most of the depopulation was not usually the direct result of policies intended at extermination or annihilation. The main reason for catastrophic population decline, in Australia and in North America, as we have seen, was disease, an unintended effect of European settler colonialism, as well as other factors such as malnutrition, alcohol and increased intertribal warfare. Yet there were also, as we have noted, intentional policies aimed at the eradication of native populations. In the end, then, we should take care, when using the term genocide in the context of colonialism, not to use it ubiquitously, but to apply it to specific examples of intentional massacres of peoples based on their belonging to membership of a particular group, such as policies towards the Pequot and Yana tribes in North America or policies towards Aboriginal peoples in Queensland in Australia in the second half of the nineteenth century, rather than labelling all colonial policy as genocide.

## Questions for Further Discussion

1   What are the connections between colonialism and genocide?

2   To what extent was settler colonialism genocidal?

The Armenians (and other Christian minorities) living in the Turkish Empire had been subjected to various forms of persecution over many centuries. Oppression of them became more acute towards the end of the nineteenth century and reached its peak with the genocide of the Armenians by the Young Turk government during the First World War. Contemporary observers of the policy of the Young Turks towards the Armenians described it as 'a massacre like none other' and 'a massacre that changes the meaning of massacre'. This suggests an unprecedented campaign of mass murder – of course, this event took place before the word 'genocide' had come into existence, yet it bore the hallmarks of a classic case of genocide. Most experts in the field concur that at least 1 million Armenians were killed in this genocide. However, differing interpretations have developed among scholars about the origins of the event and whether or not it was pre-planned, as well as about the role of the war as a factor in the genocide. One school of thought has stressed the pre-war intentions of the Young Turk leaders, as well as the primacy of their ideology. Scholars including Vahakn Dadrian have argued that the CUP planned to annihilate the Armenians before the First World War began and suggested that the war simply provided a backdrop for the genocide. In contrast, the alternative view has regarded the wartime context as crucial to the genocide, creating circumstances that resulted in what Donald Bloxham contends was a 'process of cumulative policy radicalization' in the development of a plan for destruction.[2] Raymond Kévorkian suggests that 'the physical destruction of the Armenian population of the Ottoman Empire' was a necessary part of the construction of 'a homogeneous, unified Turkish nation-state – the supreme objective of the Young Turks'.[3] He writes of two distinct but overlapping phases of the Armenian genocide: from March 1915 to April 1916, when the CUP tried to create a homogeneous region in eastern Anatolia by means of deportations; and from April to December 1916, when the CUP systematically murdered another half a million Armenians from western Anatolia and Cilicia, who had been deported to Syria and Mesopotamia. This second phase showed the intention of the CUP not just to 'cleanse' a particular area, but more decisively to eradicate the Armenians in their entirety. In contrast, rather than explaining the genocide in terms of phases, Uğur Ümit Üngör conceptualises the genocidal process as 'a three-tiered Matryoshka doll, with the tiers consisting of macro, meso, and micro levels'.[4] These layers represent the international context, the state and the ordinary people, respectively, whilst simultaneously keeping in mind the important connections between them. This perspective enables us to understand the events in a more sophisticated way, looking at the relationship between the inter-state level, the intra-societal level inside the Ottoman Empire and the micro-level of the rank-and-file executioners on the ground.

# The Historical Context

In order to understand the Armenian genocide, as Vahakn Dadrian suggests, it is necessary to comprehend the origins and evolution of the Turko-Armenian conflict.[5] Historians first noted the Armenians, an Indo-European people, at the end of the seventh century BC. The Armenians gradually came to occupy the region that today is situated in North East Turkey and the Republic of Armenia, but that during the period of our concern was located within the Ottoman Empire. Two very important characteristics separated the Armenians from the majority of the population. The first was their language, an Indo-European language, which was distinctive from the language spoken by the Turks; the second was their religion, as they had embraced Christianity from the third century AD, whilst the Turks were Muslim. These distinctions in language and religion were extremely significant. They provided the reason for hostility and sporadic persecution towards the Armenians by the Turkish population down the centuries. The Armenians were part of the multinational and multi-religious Ottoman Empire. As a Christian minority within the Muslim majority population, the Armenians had to endure an array of discriminatory measures, including special taxes levied on them. Indeed, over the centuries, many Armenians converted to Islam in order to avoid discrimination and persecution.

The Armenian population included a skilled mercantile class of prosperous traders, craftsmen and artisans, in Constantinople (Istanbul), the capital of the Ottoman Empire; some of these played a significant role in international trade. However, the Armenian community mostly consisted of tenant farmers or sharecroppers. They remained subordinated to the Turkish feudal elite over many centuries. Despite their lowly status, most Armenians lived in relative peace. They lived in a distinct community or *millet*. As the Ottoman Empire went into decline during the nineteenth century, oppression and persecution of the Armenians and other Christian minorities escalated. The disintegration of the Ottoman Empire was partly the result of its failure to modernise and compete with Western Europe. It was also due to internal corruption. These factors led to an increase in tensions within the Ottoman Empire among its various nationalities. As the Ottoman Empire began to collapse, the Armenians in particular became the victims of violent massacres, despite their assertions of loyalty to it. Unlike other of its component groups, the Armenians did not call for their autonomy from the Ottoman Empire.

However, the Armenians did undergo a period of significant cultural revival and advancement during the nineteenth century. Many travelled to Western Europe to improve their knowledge and skills and to attend universities. They established primary and secondary schools within their communities, hoping to maintain their distinctive culture by means of education. Linguistic, religious and cultural differences, exacerbated by a perceived sense that the Armenians were more economically advanced and prosperous, led to increased violence against them. Even those Armenians who worked the land adopted Western methods and were more progressive in their endeavours. Their Turkish neighbours perceived them to be more successful because of their progress and advancement, which led to economic resentment and furthered the differences between them.

Margaret Wyszomirski, one of the first scholars to write on this subject, argued:

> The status of the Armenian communities in the Ottoman Empire was precarious at best. Racially, linguistically and religiously different from the Ottoman Turks, they occupied an economic elite position in society, they began to modernise earlier than the Turks; not only was there no common value or identity between the two groups, but each had developed a brand of nationalism which excluded the other.[6]

This meant that an escalation of violence was possible with little provocation. Over the centuries, bands of marauding and pillaging Kurds, Chaldeans, Circassians and other groups had raided Armenian villages and lands. These attacks were mainly motivated by the desire for economic gain. Killings were not the primary motive, although they did occur. These plunderers were not concerned with wiping out the Armenians, but rather with the possibility of returning again and again to take more from them.

As the strength of the Ottoman Empire came to be called into question, particularly in the nineteenth century, the position of the minority populations became increasingly troubled. After the Russo-Persian War (1826–8) and the Russo-Turkish War (1828–9), Armenians, who lived on both sides of the Turkish–Russian border, came to be increasingly castigated as enemies and traitors. Bonds between Ottoman Christians and Ottoman Muslims were dissolved and the former came to be associated with the Russian 'enemy'. The Russo-Turkish War of 1828–9 had already shown 'what tenuous control the Ottomans had over their eastern borders'.[7] Towards the end of the nineteenth century, following the defeat of the Turks in the Russo-Turkish War of 1877–8, and the loss of much land to Russia, widespread massacres against the Armenian population occurred; these were carried out by Turks, but also by other communities, especially Kurds and Circassians. Article 16 of the 1878 Treaty of San Stefano obligated the Ottoman Empire to guarantee the security of the Armenians from Kurds and Circassians. Thereafter, Article 61 of the Treaty of Berlin called upon the Ottoman authorities to protect the Armenians. But the Ottoman government failed to uphold its obligations, and these guarantees to its Armenian communities were not implemented. Thomas de Waal has described how these developments made the Armenians 'dangerously dependent on the whims of the outside powers and their rivalries'.[8] Massacres of the Armenian communities by Kurds and Circassians continued. This led the Armenians to call for internal reforms to improve their conditions. Their demands, in turn, met with intransigence from the Ottoman regime. Despite (or even as a result of) British pressure on the Ottoman Empire to reform the security of the Armenians, the year 1894 saw the massacre of some 3,000 Armenians in Sassun. Britain, France and Russia once again attempted to put pressure on the

Sultan, Adbulhamid II, but the result of this was to exacerbate the situation for the Armenians in the Ottoman Empire. In October 1895, the Armenians at Trebizond on the Black Sea were massacred. This occurrence was followed by systematic attacks against Armenians in the ensuing months. These events have become known as the 'Hamidian massacres'. It is estimated that at least 200,000 Armenians were killed, thousands more were exiled and many Armenian communities were forced to convert. Lootings and burnings became commonplace. Such pogroms and massacres were Abdulhamid's way of keeping the Armenian population submissive within the existing state structure. The violence against the Armenians exemplified Abdulhamid's desperate efforts to maintain the status quo in the face of both external and internal challenges to his rule. In addition, the Great Powers were not sufficiently interested in the plight of the Armenians to intervene effectively on their behalf. Furthermore, when the Armenians did appeal to the European Christian countries, this was considered to be traitorous by the Ottoman regime, especially as the formation of Armenian revolutionary parties – such as the Armenian Revolutionary Federation Party, also known as the Dashnaks – from the 1880s onwards also caused the government concern. The Ottoman Empire used increasingly brutal methods to contain domestic troubles, especially on the part of minorities. Indeed, a growing sense of national consciousness among the Armenian population served to upset the Ottoman regime even more, as well as to arouse popular resentment among their Muslim compatriots.

However, it was the rise to power of the Young Turks – also known as the 'Ittihadists' or the Committee of Union and Progress (CUP) – that brought the greatest tragedy to the Armenians. Whilst the structural inequalities in Ottoman society had traditionally disadvantaged the Armenian communities, the new regime signalled the start of a true crisis for them. The Young Turks came to power in July 1908, quickly replacing Abdulhamid, as it became clear that he had failed to deal with the internal and external pressures faced by the Ottoman Empire. Whilst Abdulhamid had unleashed violence upon the Armenians in his efforts to maintain the status quo in which the Armenians still had a place, the Young Turks sought to bring about a fundamental change, in which the Armenians had no place at all.[9]

The scale of violence was substantially greater and the overall intention was different as well. In 1909, the Young Turks unleashed a particularly violent massacre against the Armenian population in the region of Adana in Cilicia. Richard Hovannisian estimates that between 20,000 and 30,000 Armenians were killed, as their homes were burned, plundered and raided.[10] Again, scholars have disagreed about whether or not the Hamidian massacres in the 1890s and the Adana massacres of 1909 presaged the genocide of the Armenians during the First World War. Certainly, both of these events showed the potential for wholesale massacres, large-scale violence, plunder and pillaging within the Turkish population at the end of the nineteenth century and the start of the twentieth century.

The Young Turk movement was fiercely nationalist, aiming to change the multinational Ottoman Empire into an exclusively Turkish state. Its ultra-nationalistic ideology left no room for the Armenian minority population within the borders of Turkey. Indeed, Üngör charts the origins of this Turkish nationalism back to earlier brands of European nationalism, state-building and modernisation. He argues that moves towards national unity were the product of 'social engineering', brought about forcibly when this was deemed necessary.[11] During their regime, the Young Turks strove for the creation of a new order of 'Turkism' and exclusive nationalism. In 1913, the most extreme faction of the Young Turks seized control and sought radical ways to achieve their ideological goal of exclusivist 'Turkism'. After territorial losses and military defeats, the Young Turks were determined to find a way to save the Empire. The concept of 'Turkism' promoted the ethnicity of the Turks of Anatolia, with the intention that other population groups would be excluded. This ideology was based upon a grandiose and 'mystical vision of blood and race'.[12] Ziya Gökalp was its leading ideologist. In addition, Pan-Turanian ideologue, Yusuf Akçura, called for 'the unification of the Turks – who share a language, race, customs, and even for the most part, religion, and who are spread throughout the majority of Asia and Eastern Europe'.[13] The aim of Pan-Turanianism was the unification of all Turkish people into a single empire led by the Ottoman Turks. In such an empire, the Armenians had no place. Moreover, they stood in the way geographically of the achievement of this territorial ambition. Ronald Suny suggests that rather than being a 'long-planned and carefully orchestrated' programme of annihilation, the Armenian genocide was an 'opportunistic policy to rid Anatolia of Armenians once and for all, eliminating the wedge that they provided for foreign intervention in the region, and open the way for the fantastic dream of a Turanian empire'.[14] The Young Turk government stepped up the age-old persecution of the Armenian minority to an unprecedented level. Between 1913 and 1918, the government came to be dominated by the triumvirate of Enver Pasha (Minister of War), Talaat Pasha (Minister of Internal Affairs) and Djemal Pasha (Minister of the Navy), who viewed the Armenians as a rival nationality occupying the land they considered to be Turkish.[15] The design of the Young Turks for a 'new order' in Turkey precipitated the destruction of the Armenians (and other Christian minorities in the Ottoman Empire).

The Young Turks entered the war on the German side in November 1914, in the hope that this would provide them with an opportunity to re-establish a position of regional dominance. Turkish entry into the First World War gave the CUP the chance to rid the state of undesirable components and to reorder it in line with its ideological aims and ambitions. Hence, the war transformed the nation in a way that corresponded to the conception of the ruling elite. It increased sentiments of threat and vulnerability, so that the Young Turk government had free rein to act in any way it saw fit at a time of national crisis. The government accused the Armenians of treachery and regarded them as 'enemies' to be annihilated. When Enver Pasha suffered a severe military setback in the winter of 1914–15 in the Caucasus campaign against the Russians, an excuse was formulated to scapegoat and blame the Armenians, as Russian Armenians had taken part in the campaign. This military failure led Enver Pasha to wreak revenge on the Armenian population. As Russian Armenians were fighting against Turkey, the CUP found it quite easy to convince the population that the Turkish Armenians were an active fifth column, giving information to the enemy side. The CUP portrayed the Armenians as traitors and saboteurs. Most Armenians were not disloyal to their state and did not actively support the Russians. Indeed, Donald Bloxham notes that many ordinary Ottoman Armenians were very anxious about the war with Russia.[16] The implications of potential collaboration of Ottoman Armenians with the Russians had been exemplified by the Armenian rising in Van in April 1915.[17] After this, Talaat Pasha ordered deportations on the grounds that Armenians were untrustworthy and disloyal. The British and French had landed at Gallipoli in the same month (April 1915). Within the context of the war, the CUP used the most extreme and brutal measures against the Armenian community, in the belief that there would be no repercussions, as well as having a justification for doing so. Jay Winter argues that 'total war did not produce genocide: it created the military, political, and cultural space in which it could occur'.[18]

# The Course of the Genocide, its Key Characteristics and its Effects

On 24 April 1915, 250 Armenian community leaders in Constantinople, including clergymen, politicians and writers, were arrested (many of them were subsequently killed). By removing prominent leaders, the Young Turk government intended to ensure the total subservience of the Armenian population to its deportation plans and to minimise the possibility of resistance. On 24 May 1915, an Entente statement by the French, British and Russian governments declared that they would hold criminally responsible those involved in the atrocities against the Armenians. Just three days later, on 27 May 1915, the Young Turks authorised the deportation of Armenians in the interests of 'security' and 'military necessity'.[19] This signified a state policy of community destruction. Indeed, Bloxham has argued that 'the Entente declaration was important in precipitating the general deportation programme'. He has highlighted the connection between the relationship of the Ottoman Empire with its Armenian community and the role of the European Great Powers. He states that 'the interaction between Russia and Armenian nationalists' and international factors more widely were important in the radicalisation of CUP policy.[20] On 5 June 1915, the CUP stated that it would carry out its state policy without bowing to foreign pressure or intimidation. Indeed, great power diplomacy was unable to help the Armenians resolve their status within the Ottoman Empire (see Map 3). The Great Powers were more interested in maintaining the balance of power in Europe than in the plight of the Armenians, and their attention was soon drawn to other matters.

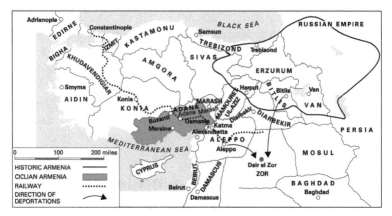

**MAP 3** *The Armenians and the Ottoman Empire, 1915.*

The genocide was carried out by means of deportation, execution (see Figure 2), starvation and exposure to the elements. This deliberately conceived governmental policy directed against the minority Armenian population ensured its segregation, isolation and exclusion. All of the Armenian communities were driven out. The Young Turk government ordered the emptying of Armenian villages and towns, forcing their inhabitants to leave their historic homes. Some travelled by train or horse-drawn wagons, but most of the Armenians went on foot. Convoys consisting mainly of women and children formed along the roads towards the Syrian desert. The government established a Commission on Immigrants in order to facilitate the 'resettlement' process. However, its true purpose was to report on the annihilation of the Armenians as they progressed on their journeys. Moreover, the regime set up a Commission on Abandoned Goods, to take possession of the property of the Armenians. This partly assisted the regime in achieving the cooperation of the rest of the population, as many gained from the situation by taking over the properties that the Armenians had been forced to leave. CUP officials also profited from the dispossession of the Armenians.[21]

The Armenians had little chance of survival even on their deportation journeys. Marauding bands and groups, including Kurdish tribesmen, stole their belongings. Indeed, the deportations were deliberately designed to force the Armenians into the open and expose them to abuse. Along the convoy routes, the Armenians were

**FIGURE 2** *Execution of Armenians.*

periodically attacked and killed by Special Organisation units. The Special Organisation was an irregular military force, first employed during the Balkan Wars and mobilised again during the First World War. At its height, it was comprised of 30,000 to 40,000 men.[22] The consistent pattern of deportation indicates the central coordination of the policies. With very little notice, towns and villages were emptied of their Armenian inhabitants. Along the way, the Armenians were robbed of their possessions and marauding bands seized Armenian women and children. The majority of the victims of this policy did not reach their final destination, being slaughtered on the way at remote locations by special killing units or dying of exposure, starvation or illness. This dispersed minority lacked the capacity for any type of resistance to their maltreatment. They were entirely at the mercy of the Turkish authorities and the Special Organisation. Those Armenians who reached the endpoint of their journey were ultimately mutilated and massacred at Deir el Zor.

In terms of its execution, the Armenian genocide was very much a state-sponsored mass murder, in which the Young Turks employed the most up-to-date technology – the telegraph service – in order to relay its messages and instructions from the Minister of War to the district governors across the land. These were then passed on to the local authorities, courts and constabularies. As Rouben Adalian has noted: 'The chain of command that put the Armenian genocide into motion joined every link in the administration of the Ottoman state.'[23] Recalcitrant officials or those that were unwilling to take part – such as the Governors-General of Kastamuni and Ankara – were simply removed from their positions. The Special Organisation, whose purpose it was to carry out mass murder, was largely made up of convicted criminals, released from prisons, who were placed into units stationed at sites along the deportation routes and destinations. They used scimitars and daggers to butcher their victims. Furthermore, the Turkish army gave weaponry to other ethnic groups and encouraged them to join in the massacres of the Armenians. Such groups raided the convoys of deportees on their journeys.

Bloxham notes that the 'very nature of the deportations is sufficient evidence of genocidal intent'.[24] Distinctions in language and religion became important in the genocide in terms of the relationship between the victims and the perpetrators and the perceptions of the perpetrators about the victims. Their hatred for the Armenians was demonstrated by the complete lack of restraint exercised by both the Turkish troops and the other bands of killers who engaged in a wide range of atrocities, such as raping women, cutting off the hands of children, herding whole groups of victims into caves, pouring in petrol and then setting them alight. Recent research has shown that sexual and gender-based violence was a significant characteristic of this genocide. Even when women and girls escaped death through forced marriage, Katharine Derderian notes that 'the ultimate result was a genocidal pattern of loss of women and children to the Armenian ethnos'.[25] Furthermore, young boys and girls were taken away, converted to Islam and Turkified in language and custom. Even the memory of the traces of existence of the Armenians was obliterated, as their churches were destroyed as well. As Peter Balakian shows: 'The CUP's destruction of churches and schools furthered the eradication of the living presence of Armenian history throughout Turkey.'[26]

How much was known about these policies? The deportations and massacres became acknowledged internationally and the massacres were widely reported at the time by journalists, diplomats and missionaries. Among other commentators, the American Ambassador to the Ottoman Empire, Henry Morganthau, described the brutal scenes of the Armenians' deportations:

The whole course of the journey became a perpetual struggle . . . Frequently anyone who dropped on the road was bayoneted on the spot. The Armenians began to die by hundreds from hunger and thirst . . . In a few days, what had been a procession of normal human beings became a stumbling horde of dust-covered skeletons, ravenously looking for scraps of food, eating any offal that came their way, crazed by the hideous sights that filled every hour of their existence, sick with all the diseases that accompany such hardships and privations, but still prodded on and on by the whips and clubs and bayonets of their executioners.[27]

How much do we know about the victims and what they endured? Survivor accounts give us an insight into first-hand experience.[28] For example, Yevnig Adrouni, an Armenian born in 1905, recalled the deportation:

They deported me . . . All the way to Deir el Zor. They did not even allow us to drink water. Along the way they took us by very narrow roads. Many of the old people who were hungry and thirsty could not walk. They used to strike them with stones and roll them down the slope.[29]

In her memoir, Vergeen Meghrouni gives a graphic depiction of her deportation by caravan, which was driven on by vicious guards, whilst being attacked by Kurdish and Turkish civilians:

Week after week, our caravan moved on . . . Even though I was becoming numb and hardened, I could not bear looking at the ghastly sights, thinking that could be Mama and me one day. Decaying corpses were often scattered all over the terrain, some half eaten by dogs and wolves, some with gaping stomachs slashed by scavenging soldiers . . . The pitiful sounds of the dying and the stench of those longer dead assailed the air for miles.[30]

The Allied powers had stated publicly that they would hold responsible all members of the Turkish government who had orchestrated or taken part in the massacres. But the perpetrators were not held to account. In October 1918, final military defeat toppled the CUP regime. Between 1915 and 1918, world leaders had made countless pledges and promises for the restitution and rehabilitation of Armenian survivors. Yet these declarations remained unfulfilled and within the space of a few years, international interest in the Armenian question waned, as did public attention and academic discourse. The mass murder of the Armenians quickly became 'the forgotten genocide'. There was no proper policy of restitution or rehabilitation for the survivors, who subsequently formed a scattered diaspora across the world, and no punishment for the perpetrators. On 5 July 1919, the CUP leadership triumvirate were condemned to death by a military tribunal – but this was *in absentia*, for they had absconded to Germany the previous year. This created a climate of impunity that only served to encourage later perpetrators of genocide. It took the most part of a century for the Armenian Catastrophe to be treated by the academic community. Eventually, Armenian survivors began to write down their testimonies and memoirs. Their personal accounts of the genocide began to encourage its study by historians and other scholars. Only comparatively recently has academic attention come to address this subject, and indeed with the centenary of the Armenian genocide in 2015, much new scholarly work and public attention has been directed to this event – and still the Turkish government persists in its denial of the Armenian genocide. Throughout all the intervening decades, the Armenian diaspora community in the USA has made a concerted effort to maintain a focus on the Armenian genocide in which their family members perished.

In addition to the genocide of the Armenians, other Christian minorities in the Ottoman Empire also perished at the hands of the CUP and its collaborators during this time, although these events are largely less well known and less discussed. For example, Hannibal Travis has demonstrated that the Assyrians of the Ottoman Empire were targeted for death comparably to the Armenians during the course of the First World War.[31] The mass killings of the Assyrians occurring concurrently with the Armenian genocide claimed the lives of an estimated 250,000 people.[32] In addition, an estimated 350,000 Greeks in the Ottoman Empire were slaughtered between 1914 and 1922.[33]

# Conclusion

Religious, linguistic and cultural differences between the Armenians and the Turks had created tensions and conflict at times between these two communities over many centuries. Dadrian notes that the 'genocidal outcome of the Turko-Armenian conflict was largely expressive of the ominously portentous manner in which the Ottoman-Turkish authorities defined, interpreted, and reacted to that conflict'.[34] The tensions between the Turks and the Armenians had increased significantly during the course of the late nineteenth century, in particular, as the Ottoman Empire came under threat. The Armenian community had experienced episodic massacres during Abdulhamid's regime. His policy, however, was not aimed at the outright elimination of the Armenians in the Ottoman Empire. It was designed to punish them for attempting to gain political and economic advancement. Even at this point, it was clear that the Ottoman Empire regarded the quest for reforms as 'a peril of existential magnitude'.[35] It was with the advent of the Young Turks, with their vehemently nationalist, exclusivist Turkic ideology, that the greatest crisis for the Armenian population occurred. Their view was of a 'new order' in which the Armenians had no place. The Armenians were perceived as threatening and inimical to the state. In the context of the First World War, the Young Turks were able to mobilise state power and the military against the Armenians, leading to their deportation and annihilation. The Special Organisation supervised and executed this extermination project. The use of technology allowed for a careful coordination of the genocidal process, with the telegraph transmission of orders. In addition, local hostility of the Turkish population and other ethnic groups, including the Kurds, was deliberately provoked and encouraged by the government and its officials. Hovannisian notes that it is possible to see 'a clear and sharp distinction between the massacres of the nineteenth century and the genocide of the twentieth century, yet also a continuum with the incremental use of unbridled violence that reached a crescendo in 1915–16'.[36]

The destruction of Armenian churches and buildings signified the intention of the regime to eliminate all remnants of the cultural heritage of the Armenians and indeed any memory of their existence in this region. The planning, coordination, scale and implementation of this killing project by the CUP made it a classic case of genocide. The Armenian genocide demonstrated what could occur when elite groups, motivated by ideological and ethnic hatred, mobilised in the context of war. This genocide, implemented during the course of the First World War, showed how easy it was for a government to create a serious and violent communally based conflict among groups who had previously lived side by side, albeit not always peacefully. The ideology of the Young Turks motivated and underpinned these wholesale massacres of the Armenian minority population in the Ottoman Empire. In terms of power relations, the odds were completely stacked against the vulnerable Armenian minority. Whether the blueprint had been created in advance or developed as the conflict progressed, the war provided the conditions in which the genocide could be carried out. The massacre of the Armenian people under the conditions of total war was a significant feature of the First World War and of the history of the twentieth century. In the next chapter, we shall turn to the subject of the Nazi genocide of the Jews.

## Questions for Further Discussion

1   Why did the Armenian genocide so quickly become 'the forgotten genocide'?

2   Why did it take so long for the Armenian genocide to be researched by historians and other scholars?

3   What was the corollary of failure to punish the perpetrators of the Armenian genocide?

4   Why does Turkey still continue to deny the Armenian genocide?

5   What has been the impact of the genocide and of this official denial on Armenian survivors and successive generations?

# Further Reading

Akçam, T., *A Shameful Act: The Armenian Genocide and the Question of Turkish Responsibility* (New York, 2006).

Akçam, T., *The Young Turks' Crime against Humanity: The Armenian Genocide and Ethnic Cleansing in the Ottoman Empire* (Princeton, NJ, 2012).

Balakian, P., *The Burning Tigris: The Armenian Genocide and America's Response* (New York, 2003).

Balakian, P., 'Raphael Lemkin, Cultural Destruction, and the Armenian Genocide', *Holocaust and Genocide Studies* Vol. 27, No. 1 (2013), pp. 57–89.

Bloxham, D., 'The Armenian Genocide of 1915–1916: Cumulative Radicalization and the Development of a Destruction Policy', *Past and Present* Vol. 181, No. 1 (2003), pp. 141–91.

Bloxham, D., *The Great Game of Genocide: Imperialism, Nationalism and the Destruction of the Ottoman Armenians* (Oxford, 2005).

Dadrian, V., 'The Secret Young-Turk Ittihadist Conference and the Decision for the World War I Genocide of the Armenians', *Holocaust and Genocide Studies* Vol. 7, No. 3 (1993), pp. 173–201.

Dadrian, V., *The History of the Armenian Genocide: Ethnic Conflict from the Balkans to Anatolia to the Caucasus* (Providence, RI, 1997).

Derderian, K., 'Common Fate, Different Experience: Gender-specific Aspects of the Armenian Genocide, 1915–1917', *Holocaust and Genocide Studies* Vol. 19, No. 1 (2005), pp. 1–25.

Graber, G., *Caravans to Oblivion: The Armenian Genocide, 1915* (New York, 1996).

Kévorkian, R., *The Armenian Genocide: A Complete History* (London, 2011).

Melson, R., *Revolution and Genocide: On the Origins of the Armenian Genocide and the Holocaust* (Chicago, IL, 1992).

Suny, R., *'They can live in the desert but nowhere else': A History of the Armenian Genocide* (Princeton, NJ, 2015).

Suny, R., Göçek, F. and Naimark, N. (eds), *A Question of Genocide: Armenians and Turks at the End of the Ottoman Empire* (New York, 2011).

Üngör, U., *The Making of Modern Turkey: Nation and State in Eastern Anatolia, 1913–1950* (Oxford, 2011).

Üngör, U. and Polatel, M., *Confiscation and Destruction: The Young Turk Seizure of Armenian Property* (London, 2011).

de Waal, T., *Great Catastrophe: Armenians and Turks in the Shadow of Genocide* (Oxford, 2015).

# 3

# The Nazi Genocide of the Jews

The word Holocaust, which means 'burnt sacrifice', came to be used from the early 1950s onwards to define the Nazi 'Final Solution' or genocide of the Jews. The Hebrew word *Shoah* (catastrophe or disaster) designates the same event. There are manifold historical debates about the genesis of the 'Final Solution' and also about the place of the Holocaust in genocide studies. The historiography of the Holocaust is vast and complex. In particular, developments in historical research since the 1990s – with the opening up of archives in Eastern Europe and the former USSR – have expanded the field considerably. In addition, the controversies between Holocaust historians and genocide scholars have made the subject even more varied and complicated. In particular, as we saw in the introduction to this book, there has been some marked enmity among certain genocide scholars towards the prominent place of the Holocaust and towards its description as 'unique'. An outline of the contours of the historiographical debates forms the first part of this chapter. The chapter then moves on to analyse the evolution and development of Nazi anti-Semitic policies between 1933 and 1945.

There can be no doubt about the centrality of anti-Semitism to Hitler's *Weltanschauung* (worldview). Hitler consistently depicted the Jewish race as the eternal enemy of the 'Aryan' race. In *Mein Kampf* (1924), Hitler had stated: 'The personification of the devil as the symbol of all evil assumes the living shape of the Jew.' Hitler's war against the Jews was a central obsession throughout his political career and one that, as Dan Michman points out, had 'a redemptive goal not just for Germany', but for the world.[1] Alon Confino too has highlighted how in the Nazi imagination, a new world could only come into existence 'without Jews'.[2] Eric Kurlander has shown, in addition, how the Nazis used images of demons, devils and other supernatural creatures to identify the Jews and figuratively transformed them into monsters in this way.[3] The Nazi 'Final Solution' enterprise called for the global elimination of 'the Jews' and of the 'Jewish spirit'. Once in power, Hitler's intense personal hatred of the Jews became central to state policy. Anti-Semitic policy and the genesis of the 'Final Solution' emerged from a number of agencies and individuals of which Hitler was just one. Throughout the period 1933–8, the development of anti-Semitic policies came from other authorities in addition to Hitler. These included: the *Gauleiter* (regional leaders) and SA (*Sturmabteilungen* or stormtroopers) using anti-Semitism between 1933 and 1935 to maintain popular morale; Joseph Goebbels, Minister of Popular Enlightenment and Propaganda, who orchestrated the Night of Broken Glass pogrom (*Reichskristallnacht*) in November 1938; and of course, the SS (*Schutzstaffeln*), whose role became increasingly important in determining anti-Semitic policy, as well as in the carrying out of the 'Final Solution'. Hitler's role in the Holocaust has been the subject of intensive historical debate over many decades. As Ian Kershaw has noted, the problem of explaining the Holocaust forms part of wider analytical interpretations of how the Nazi government functioned, especially of how decisions were made and implemented in the Third Reich.[4] These questions have challenged and vexed historians from the immediate post-war period to the present.

## The Historical Debates

Over the course of several decades of research, historians have put forward many different interpretations about the Holocaust and its genesis. During the 1970s and 1980s, there were two main lines of interpretation about the origins of the 'Final Solution'. The first was the 'intentionalist', 'Hitlerist' or 'programmatist' approach. The second was the 'structuralist' or 'functionalist' school of thought. Intentionalist historians focussed on the intentions of Hitler in determining policy direction. They proceeded from the assumption that Hitler himself from a very early date contemplated and pursued the aim to physically destroy the Jews. They showed continuity in Hitler's objectives and suggested that the 'Final Solution' was 'programmed' in advance by Hitler. Advocates of this interpretation included the historians Karl Bracher, with his emphasis on 'Hitlerism', Eberhard Jäckel, with his argument for Hitler's 'sole rule', and Klaus Hildebrand, who described the development of 'Hitler's programmatic ideas about the destruction of the Jews'. Gerald Fleming is most noted for his argument that 'a straight path' led from Hitler's personal anti-Semitism to his liquidation orders during the war.[5] Fleming argued that there was an unwavering continuity of aim in Nazi anti-Semitic policy, and suggested that Hitler developed 'a strategic plan for the realisation of his political aim' at the beginning of the 1920s. Lucy Dawidowicz concluded that from 1918 onwards, there had never been 'any ideological deviation or wavering determination' in Hitler's plans for the Jews.[6]

In contrast, structuralist or functionalist historians focussed on the fragmented decision-making processes of the Nazi bureaucracy. They showed that the Nazi state and administration was rather chaotic and unwieldy in nature and that Nazi policies towards the Jews were improvised and unsystematic. Most notably, Karl Schleunes argued that the 'road to Auschwitz' was 'twisted'.[7] He suggested that Hitler's hand appeared only rarely in the making of anti-Semitic policies between 1933 and 1938, and stated: 'The Final Solution as it emerged in 1941 and 1942 was not the product of a grand design.' Martin Broszat similarly contended that the 'Final Solution' was not planned or programmed in advance, and Hans Mommsen concurred about the absence of clear planning and direction from Hitler. Mommsen argued that the fragmented decision-making process in the Third Reich led to 'cumulative radicalisation' in the evolution of the 'Final Solution'. Structuralist historians thus explained the origins of the 'Final Solution' in Poland as a response to a 'crisis from below' and an escalation of policy into 'cumulative radicalisation', rather than as a result of Hitler's personal obsession with the Jews. In part, this was manifested, for example, by the rivalry between the *Gauleiter* Arthur Greiser of the Warthegau region and Hans Frank of the General Government region. The rivalry between them to interpret Hitler's will created a radicalisation of measures against the Jews in the absence of a clear policy line coming from above. They justified their actions in terms of working towards the will of the *Führer*, despite or even because of the absence of a *Führer* order.

Any investigation of the Third Reich and the Holocaust must consider the complexities of life and death, as well as the functioning and complex process of decision-making of the brutal Nazi dictatorship. We can undoubtedly determine Hitler's important role in the genocide of the Jews, but must also take into account a wider group of those responsible, including Goering, Heydrich and Himmler, among other key Nazi leaders, the *SS-Einsatzgruppen*, the *Gauleiter*, even civil servants, as well as all the people and organisations involved in transportation and killing the Jews of Europe at the death camps. Furthermore, recent research has shown an even wider web of complicity deriving from the opportunities that the pillaging of Jewish property presented for the Nazis, for ordinary Germans and others. These possibilities, in turn, strengthened support for the regime. Encouraging local populations to plunder Jewish property brought them into complicity with the regime, its persecution and its genocide. Jews became fair game and an economic resource to be exploited. In this regard, greed was critical. German-orchestrated plunder meant that those who enriched themselves at the expense of the Jews became increasingly associated with and complicit in the crimes of the Nazi system. Collaboration was much more widespread and varied than had previously been understood. Greed and corruption were significant motivating factors in anti-Semitic activities. David Cesarani has highlighted the extent to which the economic exploitation of the Jews, the expropriation of their homes and assets, benefited the German population, as well as the allies and collaborators of the Nazis. This widens the circle of those who stood to gain from the persecution and genocide of the Jews. Cesarani has called into question the idea of bystanders as passive spectators and shown that many were complicit as they had much to gain.[8] Plunder, ritualised violence and brutality against Jewish populations in newly occupied territories was a key characteristic of Nazi expansion. Every stage in the expansion of the Third Reich, from the *Anschluss* (union) with Austria in 1938 onwards, was marked by brutal violence against Jewish populations. These actions in turn radicalised attitudes and practices. The position of the Jews deteriorated sharply once the war began, as the abuse and mass shootings of Jews in Poland and the USSR marked a deepening escalation of violence accompanied by a weakening of inhibitions.

The nature of the sources, as well as the deliberately unclear language used to refer to the killing operations, has led historians to draw very different conclusions about the timing and the nature of the decision to annihilate the Jews. These varied interpretations by leading experts show that the evidence for the precise nature of a decision to implement the 'Final Solution', as well as for its timing, is circumstantial. Hitler did not need to issue directives or take clear initiatives in the Jewish question between 1939 and 1941. Here, the momentum sustained itself by a combination of bureaucratic measures and initiatives taken by other organisations and individuals. As Kershaw notes, Hitler's 'own direct role was largely confined to the propaganda arena – to public tirades of hatred'.[9] Indeed, the summer and autumn of 1941 were characterised by much confusion and lack of coordination in anti-Semitic policy. No single decision brought about the 'Final Solution'. A lengthy process of radicalisation characterised the search for a 'solution to the Jewish question'. Hitler's approval of the killing of the Jews is not in doubt, but his precise role in these key phases of the escalation of policy remains, as Christian Gerlach has noted, mainly in the shadows. Whilst Hitler may not have instigated the key steps into genocide – central direction came mainly from the Reich Security Head Office (*Reichssicherheitshauptamt* or RSHA) – he certainly authorised them. The nature of charismatic rule in Nazi Germany is an important part of the explanation for the Holocaust, because it shows how Hitler's intention was interpreted and the momentum for an escalation in anti-Semitic policies was sustained partly through a desire of Nazi leaders and organisations to please the *Führer* and carry out his wishes.

A distinct enlargement in the already vast field of Holocaust studies historiography, in particular since the 1990s, has engendered a number of significant shifts in our knowledge and in interpretation. Whilst it is not possible to cover all aspects of this large and varied literature here, it is important to signpost the extent of this scholarly research and its consequences for our understanding of the 'Final Solution'. Research into primary sources that became available after the fall of the USSR and the Communist bloc in Eastern Europe has resulted in a shift in perceptions of decision-making in relation to the 'Final Solution'. Building on the issues that had preoccupied historians who supported the intentionalist and functionalist interpretations, the newly accessed documents in Eastern Europe led to the discussion of a different set of questions: What was the relationship between the centre and the periphery in decision-making for the 'Final Solution'? To what extent was the 'Final Solution' the result of top-down decision-making processes and to what extent did ad hoc decisions in a variety of locations on the ground cause the process of the 'Final Solution' to develop? Recent research has shown that a wide variety of German administrative and military authorities used ad hoc solutions to unanticipated problems they faced in regard to the 'Jewish question' at grass-roots level. And so a two-way process occurred, with improvised decisions and actions taken at ground level, as well as new directives and orders coming from the central authorities in Berlin. New scholarly debate has focussed on the extent to which the centre or the periphery moved Nazi policy forward to the 'Final Solution'. Christian Gerlach has argued that the mass murder of Jews in the USSR came about through issues of food and supply scarcity on the ground, rather than being driven by ideology. Other historians have emphasised central, top-down policy and the ideological fear of 'Judeo-Bolshevism' as the impetus for the 'Final Solution'. Despite persistent differences of opinion among scholars on a number of issues, these historiographical developments have shifted the perception of the genesis of the 'Final Solution' as a policy that was shaped gradually and that crystallised through many grass-roots level initiatives into a 'programme' of genocide.

There has also been considerable debate about the way in which the terms Holocaust and genocide relate to each other. The fields of both Holocaust history and genocide studies are very large, complex and ever growing, as new research pushes forward the boundaries of knowledge. Many developments in these fields of research have been very useful in enhancing our understanding of a whole gamut of historical events. However, a particularly heated debate about the place of the Holocaust in genocide studies has created some impasses. Part of the difficulty lies in the distinctions between the approaches of various academic disciplines – for example, historians come to the subject in a different way to social scientists. This has led to some controversial disputes, which make already complicated issues sometimes even more obscure or difficult to comprehend. Yehuda Bauer highlighted the unique features of the Holocaust as a tragedy of the Jewish people, whilst at the same time acknowledging its universal implications for mankind. He subsequently moved away from the concept of uniqueness, to state that the Holocaust was 'unprecedented but by no means unique'. Certainly, as many other experts have concurred, it did contain unprecedented elements, not least the role of Nazi ideology. And so differences of interpretation among scholars abound. Genocide scholar Colin Tatz argues that 'our maturing discipline needs to find a sense of collegiality, consensus on terminology, and yardsticks with which to measure scales, dimensions, and degrees of the crime'. He writes: 'Foremost is the challenge of finding a space for encompassing and embracing the Holocaust with some comfort . . . The judeocide is an ally, not an enemy, and not on the margins.'[10]

The recent emphasis in Holocaust historiography has moved away from Auschwitz to other killing sites in Eastern Europe, where more than 2.5 million Jews were brutally murdered. Mass shootings by the Nazis, their allies and collaborators accounted for a significant part of the total death toll. Auschwitz was not representative of the whole Holocaust, as so much of the killing was carried out in other ways, by a host of ordinary people – the Holocaust was not limited to modern industrialised mass murder. The new research on Eastern Europe has challenged Auschwitz-centred explanations. Whilst Auschwitz and the other death camps fitted into 'modernity' interpretations of the Holocaust, such as those put forward by Zygmunt Bauman, the killing of the Jews on the ground by the *SS-Einsatzgruppen*, the *Wehrmacht* (armed forces), as well as by non-German collaborators, is not covered by such explanations.[11]

Whilst the weight of earlier research until the late 1980s had been on ideology, structures, leaders and institutions, the *Historikerstreit* (historians' debate) in West Germany created a significant change in interpretations and engendered a deeper study of German society as a whole during the Nazi period. Furthermore, scholarship has highlighted a broad gamut of local administrators, educators, planners, engineers and academics, among other social and professional sectors in German society, who enabled the Nazi enterprise. Daniel Goldhagen's controversial book in 1996 intensified these developments.[12] Newer research has uncovered the wide and willing complicity of Germans and Austrians, but also populations in other European countries, such as Hungary and Croatia, who benefited from Nazi anti-Semitic policies. Furthermore, research on the voices of both perpetrators and victims through their written narratives has added an extra angle to our knowledge and understanding of the Holocaust. Recent scholarship has also investigated the dividing line between perpetrators and bystanders. In particular, it has pointed out the wide array of complicitors and enablers in German and Austrian society. It has become clear that individuals who would previously have been described as 'bystanders' were in fact part of the perpetrator category.[13] Hence, significant developments in Holocaust research since 1990 have changed our understanding of this key historical event. Interpretations of central issues have altered considerably. A comprehension of the dynamics of individual and institutional behaviour has expanded scholarship of many aspects of the 'Final Solution', even though this has not always been replicated in popular representations of the Holocaust.

# Nazi Anti-Semitic Policies and the 'Final Solution'

Christopher Browning states that the Holocaust entails 'the total historical experience of the Nazi persecution of the Jews, culminating in the Final Solution'. Certainly, an examination of Nazi policy throughout the entire period from 1933 to 1945 is necessary to our understanding of the Holocaust. When Hitler came to power, there were approximately half a million Jews living in Germany. The Jews were persecuted by the Nazi regime from its very earliest days in power. Nazi anti-Semitism differed from earlier forms of anti-Semitism. Traditional anti-Semitism, a phenomenon that had existed in Europe over many centuries, was largely religious in character. It opposed Jews because they rejected Christianity. Traditional anti-Semitism held that if a Jew converted to Christianity, then he or she could be saved. A new brand of anti-Semitism had emerged during the second half of the nineteenth century, influenced by Social

Darwinism and racial theories, which was much more radical and uncompromising. It was based upon the definition of the Jews as a 'race'. Hence, there could be no salvation through conversion to Christianity. Hitler was highly influenced by racial anti-Semitism, a phenomenon that had grown in influence in Germany in the years following the First World War and formed the basis of the Nazis' racial ideology. As Nazi policy was based upon racial anti-Semitism, all Jews – whether or not they practised their religion – were subjected to persecution by the regime.

Policies designed to persecute Germany's Jews and to segregate them from the rest of society began with the national boycott of Jewish businesses on 1 April 1933, which set the stage for their economic harassment. The boycott was instigated by Party radicals, in particular members of the SA, who were euphoric after the Nazi Party's 'seizure of power'. Posters and placards were put up outside Jewish shops and businesses, saying: 'Germans defend yourselves! Do not buy from Jews!' SA men placed themselves in front of Jewish shops to deter customers. The boycott was intended to become a permanent feature of life in the Third Reich, but because many Germans ignored the SA men and the posters, and continued to buy from Jewish shops, it was abandoned after a day. The first legal measure against the Jews was implemented within a week of the boycott. On 7 April 1933, Clause 3 of the Law for the Restoration of the Professional Civil Service called for the 'retirement' of Jewish officials from their positions. By May 1933, all 'non-Aryan' public sector employees were dismissed from their jobs. After this, the range of professions and occupations from which Jews were excluded gradually widened. These legal measures were accompanied by informal social ostracism. Jews were at first encouraged and later obliged to give up their membership of clubs and organisations.

The Nuremberg Laws of 15 September 1935 were comprised of two edicts designed to segregate Jews from the rest of society. The Reich Citizenship Law denied Jews their equal civil rights, redefining them as 'subjects' instead of 'citizens'. The Law for the Protection of German Blood and Honour prohibited marriages and sexual relationships between Jews and 'Aryans'. The significance of the Nuremberg Laws was their creation of a legal separation between Jews and the rest of German society. When they were passed, many

Jews saw the Nuremberg Laws as a definitive clarification of their social and legal position. They believed that if they lived within the parameters defined by them, the violence and illegal persecution would cease. This may explain why the number of Jews seeking to emigrate temporarily dropped after the Nuremberg Laws were passed. But the Nuremberg Laws, in reality, brought about a grave deterioration in the situation of most Jews and had a considerable impact upon how Jews came to be regarded by their 'Aryan' compatriots.

Between 1936 and 1937, the pace of anti-Semitic legislation appeared to decelerate and no major initiatives were taken with regard to the 'Jewish question'. For example, during the 1936 Berlin Olympic Games, anti-Semitic posters were temporarily taken down, so as not to draw attention to the anti-Semitic nature of the regime to foreign visitors and commentators. Yet new decrees were still passed that marginalised Jews both from the economy and from society. A host of other measures were employed and laws passed to isolate and humiliate the Jews and to separate them physically from the rest of the population. For example, in July 1938, streets named after Jews were renamed and park benches were designated 'for Aryans only'. In the same month, the approximately 3,000 Jewish doctors still practising their profession were prohibited from doing so. Only 709 were allowed to maintain their practices, but were designated as 'medical practitioners' to Jewish patients only. In September 1938, only 172 lawyers were allowed to continue in their profession, and they were similarly designated as 'legal counsel' to Jewish clients only. By November 1938, Jews were prohibited from going to the theatre, concerts and exhibitions. They were also excluded from certain restaurants. With each successive anti-Semitic measure, contacts between Jews and 'Aryans' were minimised, formalised or banned, leading to a spatial separation or exclusion of the Jews from the rest of German society. The Jews were systematically and deliberately pauperised in a process known as the 'Aryanisation of the economy', which excluded Jews from employment and forced them to sell or close down their businesses.

Nazi anti-Semitic policy shifted gear on the night of 9–10 November 1938, when Goebbels unleashed a pogrom known as *Reichskristallnacht* ('The Night of Broken Glass'). Goebbels used the murder of Ernst vom Rath, a German official in Paris, by a young Polish Jew, Hershel Grynspan, as a pretext for the pogrom. *Reichskristallnacht* represented a decisive turning point in Nazi anti-Semitic policy. It was an unprecedented, widespread and violent act of persecution that took place in full view of the German public. Some 7,000 Jewish businesses were destroyed, almost every synagogue in the country was burned down, 26,000 Jewish men were sent to concentration camps and ninety-one people were killed during the course of the pogrom. Fire brigades were instructed not to extinguish fires in Jewish properties. Goebbels claimed that the pogrom was a 'spontaneous popular response' on the part of the German nation to the murder of vom Rath, but it was, in reality, a centrally planned and orchestrated action.

Following *Reichskristallnacht*, Hermann Goering held a meeting on 12 November 1938, at which he told top government and Party officials that the 'Jewish question' had to be settled: 'now, once and for all, coordinated and solved in one way or another'. In the aftermath of this meeting, the 'solution to the Jewish question' was placed in the hands of the SS. Jews were now to be totally excluded from the economy in accordance with the Decree for the Exclusion of Jews from German Economic Life. On 15 November, the Ministry of Education banned all Jewish children from state schools. On 3 December, German Jews had their driving licences revoked. By the beginning of 1939, it was becoming clear that policy was aimed at the compulsory emigration of Jews, in order to make the German Reich *judenfrei* (free of Jews). To this end, Goering ordered Heydrich to establish a centre for Jewish emigration. However, Jews who left Germany were obliged to pay a hefty 'flight tax'.

Racial purity, the concept of the *Herrenvolk* (master race) and anti-Semitism were core aspects of Nazi ideology. Both before and during the war, the Nazi regime deliberately built upon and also created popular mistrust towards the Jews by means of propaganda – in particular, through the use of posters, as well as *Der Stürmer*, an anti-Semitic journal published under the aegis of Julius Streicher, the *Gauleiter* of Franconia. Ernst Hiemer's children's book, *The Poisonous Mushroom* (1938), employed a whole array of anti-Semitic imagery, with caricatures, graphic illustrations and vivid descriptions of Jews as hideous, hook-nosed seducers of 'Aryan' women, Christ-slayers and money-grabbing usurers. In addition, a trilogy of films about the Jews was screened in 1940 – *Die Rothschilds* (The Rothschilds), *Jud Süss* (Jew Süss) and *Der ewige Jude* (The Eternal Jew). The first of these, *Die Rothschilds*, was an attempt to explain the rise to power and wealth of the Rothschild family, a prominent Jewish banking family, and the emergence of the 'Jewish British plutocracy'. It revealed the 'historical fact' that Jewish financiers had profited from the death of German soldiers. *Jud Süss* depicted the inherent rootlessness of the Jew and his ability to assimilate himself into any society. Eric Rentschler has shown that in 'constructing a malevolent other, Nazi propagandists insisted that they were serving the public good by revealing the Jew's true face'.[14] This film unquestionably contributed to the anti-Semitism already prevalent in Germany, for it brought together archetypes and themes that created the desired antipathy towards the Jews under the guise of entertainment that resulted in great box office success. Rentschler notes that 'it not only confirmed existing prejudices; it agitated, militated, and called for action'.[15] *Der ewige Jude* covered the entire gamut of Nazi allegations against the Jews. It was one of the most virulent and effective propaganda films ever made. By associating Jews with rats, the audience was led to believe that they were disease bearers and subhuman. In addition, the Jews were portrayed as a racial and economic threat, as was the case in so many examples of Nazi anti-Semitic propaganda. This propaganda was designed to rationalise the extermination of the Jews as expressed in Hitler's *Mein Kampf* and in his speeches.

In his 30 January 1939 Reichstag speech, Hitler declared the Jews as the enemies of National Socialism and argued that if they did not break away from their parasitic lives, they risked 'a crisis of unimaginable proportions'. He made a prophecy that:

> If the international Jewish financiers in and outside Europe should succeed in plunging the nations once more into a world war, then the result will not be the Bolshevising of the earth, and thus a victory of Jewry, but the annihilation of the Jewish race in Europe.

It is worth noting here that emigration was still the policy being pursued by the National Socialist regime at this time. However,

Germany's Jews were additionally subjected to more and more restrictions on their lives throughout the course of 1939, and the outbreak of war in September 1939 was significant in the development of Nazi anti-Semitic policy. The speedy conquest of Poland led to a transformation of the 'Jewish question'. Emigration was no longer a realistic policy aim. By June 1940, Heydrich stated that the 'overall problem' could not be solved by emigration. 'Territorial solutions' such as the Nisko Project and the Madagascar Plan were proposed. It was hoped that in such remote locations, the Jews would be eradicated, but neither of these plans were realised. The Nazis established ghettoes in Poland, as a temporary arrangement, but these engendered a host of administrative problems. At first, the ghettoes were used to concentrate the Jewish population into forced areas within the larger cities, such as Warsaw and Łódź. As conditions in the ghettoes worsened, Nazi policy became increasingly radicalised. The ghettoisation, Cesarani contends, was 'muddled and inconsistently implemented'.[16] Wolfgang Benz has described the function of the ghettoes between 1940 and 1943: 'they were the waiting rooms of destruction, the antechambers of hell, the stations on the way to the camps to which human beings were deported for the express purpose of being murdered.'[17]

With the German invasion of the Soviet Union, Operation Barbarossa (22 June 1941), the 'solution to the Jewish question' entered yet another phase. The *SS-Einsatzgruppen* followed in the wake of the *Wehrmacht* as it penetrated Soviet territory, waging an unprecedented campaign of mass murder against the Jewish population. Heydrich's *Kommissarbefehl* (Commissar Order) of 2 July 1941, ordering that communist officials, Jews in Party and State employment and other radical elements were to be executed, gave the go-ahead to the *SS-Einsatzgruppen* to kill all Jews they encountered, including women and children. Mass shootings of Jews occurred throughout the Soviet territories occupied by the Nazis – in eastern Poland, Latvia, Estonia, Lithuania, Byelorussia, Ukraine and the Crimea. The actions of the *SS-Einsatzgruppen* marked a sharp radicalisation in Nazi anti-Semitic policy.

In the meantime, on 31 July 1941, Goering ordered Heydrich to make 'all necessary preparations with regard to organisational, technical and material matters for bringing about a complete solution of the Jewish question within the German sphere of influence in Europe'. From 1 September 1941, the German Jews were forced to wear the Yellow Star, to mark them out, once and for all, from the rest of the German population. This visible distinction signified their total exclusion and made them more easily identifiable for later deportation. On 23 October 1941, Himmler ordered that no more Jews were allowed to emigrate from anywhere inside Germany or Nazi-occupied Europe. This was an important signal, as Jewish emigration had been a previous goal of the Nazi regime. German Jews were deported to death camps in Poland where they shared the fate of the rest of European Jewry in the Nazis' systematic extermination process: the 'Final Solution' (see Figure 3).

Whilst Götz Aly points to 'clear steps in development' of a decision for genocide in March, July and October 1941, Christian Gerlach suggests that a 'basic decision' by Hitler to destroy all European Jewry was taken at a meeting of his regional leaders on 12 December 1941, the day after Germany's declaration of war on the USA. From the late summer, throughout the autumn and winter of 1941, a number of experiments and 'local initiatives' were taken to kill Jews. For example, in December 1941, the first gassings were carried out

**FIGURE 3** *Arrival of Jewish deportees at Auschwitz, May 1944.*

at Chelmno in Poland. Hence, centralised administrative control over killing Jews was only achieved retrospectively, after localised killings had begun. This was the function of the Wannsee Conference on 20 January 1942.[18] Mark Roseman has shown that the Wannsee Conference was a powerfully symbolic event:

Here was the distinguished ambience of an elegant villa, in a cultivated suburb, in one of Europe's most sophisticated capitals. Here were fifteen educated, civilised bureaucrats, from an educated, civilised society, observing all due decorum. And here was genocide, going through, on the nod.[19]

Cesarani argued that the Nazi genocide of the Jews, as it emerged from the spring of 1942 onwards, 'was no less haphazard than previous phases of anti-Jewish policy'.[20] Michman concurs that policies 'evolved through zigzags, with the bureaucracy sometimes moving in contrary directions based on differing interpretations of Hitler's will'.[21] Cesarani has shown how the 'Final Solution' – as a pan-European project – evolved slowly and erratically after the Wannsee Conference in January 1942. He has described it as 'low-cost and low-tech'.[22] Nevertheless, the contingencies of the war and the need to solve problems on the ground influenced Nazi decision-making in regard to the deployment of the 'Final Solution of the Jewish Question'.

The Jews were murdered at six camps in Poland established expressly for this purpose: Chelmno, Bełżec, Sobibór and Treblinka were solely extermination camps; Majdanek and Auschwitz, were dual purpose camps, functioning as forced labour and death camps (see Map 4). The extermination-only camps were small in area compared to Auschwitz because of the absence of associated labour camps. Between 1942 and 1945, industrialised mass murder on an unprecedented scale took place at these extermination camps.[23] Survivor testimonies from Auschwitz give us clear indications about the intentions of the Nazis and the conditions in this camp. Livia Bitton-Jackson compares herself after her arrival at Auschwitz with inmates who had been there longer:

The strange creatures we saw as we entered the camp, the shaven, grey-cloaked bunch who ran to the barbed wire to stare at

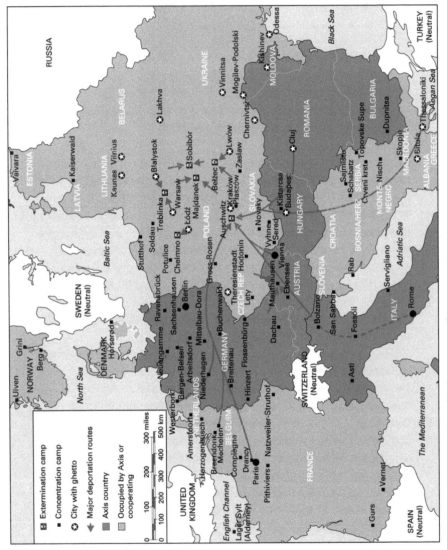

**MAP 4** *Nazi death camps and concentration camps.*

us, we are them! We look exactly like them. Same bodies, same dresses, same blank stares. They, too, must have arrived from home recently. They, too, were ripe women and young girls, bewildered and bruised. They too longed for dignity and compassion. And they, too, were transformed into figures of contempt instead.[24]

Elie Wiesel also describes the impact of the arrival rituals: 'in a few seconds, we had ceased to be men. Had the situation not been so tragic, we might have laughed . . . I too had become a different person.'[25] And this was only the beginning. An account from Auschwitz survivor, Shlomo Venezia, who worked in the *Sonderkommando* (the special detachments that emptied the gas chambers and cremated the bodies of the victims), noted: 'It was a foul, filthy death. A forced death, difficult and experienced differently by each of them . . . The sight that lay before us when we opened the door was terrible; nobody can ever imagine what it was like.'[26]

Towards the end of the war, the inmates of Auschwitz and other camps faced extremely long, arduous and perilous 'death marches', as the Nazis attempted to empty out remaining victims from the death camps and destroy evidence of their exterminatory policies. Subsequently, whilst liberation came in 1945, the misery of the Jews did not end neatly in that year.[27] Many thousands were placed into 'displaced persons' camps. Jewish victims did not receive restitution and reparation in the immediate aftermath of the war and there was, as Cesarani has noted, 'much unfinished business'.[28]

# Conclusion

The responsibility for the 'Final Solution' extended much beyond Hitler. We have seen the roles of Goering, Heydrich and Himmler, among other key Nazi leaders, the *SS-Einsatzgruppen*, the *Gauleiter*, even civil servants and physicians. As Michman notes:

Hitler's visions of the need to combat *der Jude* and the global threat of *das Judentum* took shape through trial and error in which broadening circles played a role. These circles included not only the German bureaucracy . . . [b]ut many beyond it, first in Germany, later in every occupied and allied country.[29]

It is necessary to take into account all the people and organisations involved in the transportation and the killing the Jews of Europe at the death camps – from the provision of a vast network of train transportation to the chemical company that produced the Zyklon B for the gas chambers, as well as many others that organised and administered the Nazi camps. Complicity extends too, as we have seen, to the many who stood to gain from the economic plunder of Jewish assets and possessions. In the end, through the use of mass shootings and death camps, the Nazis' 'Final Solution', carried out as a pan-European project of genocide, took the lives of some 6 million European Jews. The next chapter explores the Nazi genocide of the Sinti and Roma.

## Questions for Further Discussion

1   To what extent was the Holocaust unique or paradigmatic?

2   How did Nazi anti-Semitism differ from Christian anti-Semitism and what effect did this have on Nazi policies?

3   How did the Nazis carry out the 'Final Solution'?

4   How have historical debates about the Holocaust and its origins changed over the decades?

5   Why has there been so much debate between Holocaust historians and genocide scholars?

## Further Reading

Bajohr, F., 'Aryanisation' in Hamburg: The Economic Exclusion of Jews and the Confiscation of their Property in Nazi Germany (New York and Oxford, 2002).
Bankier, D. (ed.), Probing the Depths of German Antisemitism: German Society and the Persecution of the Jews, 1933–1941 (New York, 2000).

Barkai, A., *From Boycott to Annihilation: The Economic Struggle of German Jews, 1933–1943* (London, 1989).

Browning, C., *The Origins of the Final Solution: The Evolution of Nazi Jewish Policy, September 1939 – March 1942* (Lincoln, NE, 2004).

Cesarani, D., *Final Solution: The Fate of the Jews 1933–49* (London, 2016).

Confino, A., *Foundational Pasts: The Holocaust as Historical Understanding* (New York, 2012).

Dean, M., *Robbing the Jews: The Confiscation of Jewish Property in the Holocaust, 1933–1945* (New York, 2008).

Friedländer, S., *Nazi Germany and the Jews: The Years of Persecution, 1933–1939* (London, 1997).

Friedländer, S., *Nazi Germany and the Jews: The Years of Extermination, 1939–1945* (London, 2007).

Gerlach, C., *The Extermination of the European Jews* (Cambridge, 2016).

Griech-Polelle, B., *Anti-Semitism and the Holocaust: Language, Rhetoric and the Tradition of Hatred* (London, 2017).

Hayes, P. and Roth, J. (eds), *The Oxford Handbook of Holocaust Studies* (Oxford, 2011).

Kaplan, M., *Between Dignity and Despair: Jewish Life in Nazi Germany* (Oxford, 1998).

Lawson, T., *Debates on the Holocaust* (Manchester, 2010).

Michman, D., *Holocaust Historiography: A Jewish Perspective. Conceptualization, Terminology, Approaches and Fundamental Issues* (London, 2003).

Nicosia, F. and Scrase, D. (eds), *Jewish Life in Nazi Germany: Dilemmas and Responses* (New York and Oxford, 2010).

Roseman, M., *The Villa, the Lake, the Meeting: Wannsee and the Final Solution* (London, 2003).

Stone, D., *Histories of the Holocaust* (Oxford, 2010).

# 4

# The Nazi Genocide of the Sinti and Roma

The Sinti and Roma ('Gypsies') remained forgotten victims of National Socialism for many decades. The Nazi perpetration of the genocide of the European Sinti and Roma population was not widely recognised until the 1980s. Why were they forgotten for so long? What implications did this have on historical scholarly debate, as well as public knowledge of this aspect of the Second World War? Why has there been a tendency to lump together all Nazi victims under the heading of the Holocaust? It is certainly inaccurate to do this. Whilst the Jews were undoubtedly and undeniably the largest group of victims of Nazi policy, as we saw in the previous chapter, the Sinti and Roma faced a genocide of their own at the hands of the Nazis. Ian Hancock rightly contends that the history of the Sinti and Roma must be 'presented in its own context, and not as a corollary to that of another people'.[1]

Hitler himself had very little interest in the 'Gypsies'. They were not the subject of his speeches and tirades in the way that the Jews were. This indication that the Sinti and Roma were not a high priority to the Nazi regime has had important implications for the historiography of the Sinti and Roma under National Socialism. In the early post-war period, the Nazi persecution and murder of the Sinti and Roma was scarcely mentioned. The few publications that touched upon the subject were the survivor autobiographies and memoirs of Jews and former political prisoners, which made passing references to the Nazi persecution and murder of the Sinti and Roma. Sinti and Roma survivors either could not tell their own stories or did not want to. The experience of the Sinti and Roma in the Third Reich was not the subject of scholarly interest until much later.

Donald Kenrick and Grattan Puxon published the first overall study of the Nazi persecution of the Sinti and Roma, *The Destiny of Europe's Gypsies*, in 1972.[2] This was followed by research in the 1980s and 1990s, which began to document the history of the Sinti and Roma in the Nazi era much more fully. There have been interviews with survivors, allowing those who were unable to write to have their stories told, or providing those who were unwilling to tell their stories at first with the opportunity to tell them after the passage of some time. In recent years, some Sinti and Roma survivors have published their own autobiographical accounts. These developments have allowed historians to consider not only the Nazi policy-making process, but also the dreadful consequences for the victims of the policy.[3]

# Context: Anti-'Gypsy' Discrimination and Policies Before the Nazi Era

Similarly to the Jews, the 'Gypsies' had been subjected to discrimination and persecution over many centuries. The 'Gypsies' had originated in Northern India and migrated across Asia westwards into Europe between the fifth and eleventh centuries. By the time they arrived in Europe, most of the land was already under ownership, which made it hard for the newcomers to establish permanent settlements. They moved across the countryside, living off the land. They were viewed with suspicion on account of their dark skin and nomadic lifestyle. The Persian poet, Firdausi, had written in the tenth century: 'No washing ever whitens the black Gypsy.'[4] Discrimination, scapegoating and oppression marked the history of the Sinti and Roma throughout the following centuries.

The 'Gypsies' were accused of cannibalism, of spreading dirt and disease, and of being spies, sorcerers, swindlers, thieves, beggars and tricksters. Throughout the medieval and early modern period, various attempts were made to expel the 'Gypsies' or to assimilate them. The churches and trade guilds had an unfavourable attitude towards the 'Gypsies', but some noblemen invited 'Gypsy' musicians and entertainers into their homes and sometimes protected them from repressive laws, offering them refuge on their estates. In Western Europe, the Sinti (see Figure 4) were eventually tolerated as migratory workers and partially integrated into the host lands, but the wandering Roma eluded assimilation, despite various prohibitions against their nomadism, clothing, music and language. 'Gypsies' were subjected to torture and punishment by the authorities, as well as 'gypsy hunts', a popular sport in a number of European lands, including Germany and Holland.[5] Myths about the 'Gypsies' portrayed them at best as 'noble savages', but more often as 'brutes'. There were contradictions between these 'Gypsy myths' and the way of life and culture of the Sinti and Roma, yet suspicion and dislike of the 'Gypsies' persisted into the modern era (and indeed continues to this day).

German 'Gypsy' policy-making in the late nineteenth century and early twentieth century was permeated by 'Gypsy' myths and stereotypes, and sought to introduce measures to combat the *Zigeunerplage* ('Gypsy Plague'). These measures provided a foundation for subsequent Nazi 'Gypsy' policy. In Bavaria, the security

**FIGURE 4** *German Sinti in Berlin, 1929.*

police had kept a central register on 'Gypsies' since 1899. After 1911, these records included fingerprints. On 16 July 1926, Bavaria introduced a Law for the Combating of Gypsies, Travellers and the Workshy. It stated that 'Gypsies and persons who roam about in the manner of Gypsies may only itinerate with wagons and caravans if they have permission from the police authorities'. This permission was only granted for a maximum of one calendar year and was revocable at any time. It had to be presented on demand to the police. The law further stated that:

> Gypsies and travellers may not roam about or camp in bands. The association of several single persons or several families, and the association of single persons with a family to which they do not belong, is to be regarded as constituting a band. A group of persons living together like a family is also to be regarded as a band.[6]

'Gypsies' were only allowed to park their wagons and caravans on open-air sites designated by the local police authorities and only for a specified period of time. Furthermore, the law ruled that they could be sent to workhouses for up to two years if they could not prove to be in regular paid employment.

## Nazi Anti-'Gypsy' Policies

Once the Nazis came to power, the persecution of the Sinti and Roma was centralised and policies against them became increasingly radicalised. The 'Gypsies', approximately 35,000 in number, made up only 0.05 per cent of the German population in 1933.[7] They were considered to be marginal, inferior, criminal and unproductive. Such stereotypes provided the justification for their social exclusion in the Third Reich. The 'Gypsies' were already marginalised, but the Nazi regime intensified their persecution. A number of new Nazi decrees had an early impact upon Germany's 'Gypsies'. They were forcibly sterilised under the 1933 Law for the Prevention of Hereditarily Diseased Offspring and castrated under the 1933 Law against Dangerous Habitual Criminals. The 1933 Denaturalisation Law and

1934 Expulsion Law forced stateless and foreign Sinti and Roma to leave Germany. Early measures also included the arrest and detainment of 'Gypsies' in concentration camps.

Sybil Milton has described how a 'decentralised patchwork of parallel local decrees provided the prototype for the synchronisation and radicalisation of measures against Roma and Sinti throughout the Reich after 1935'.[8] In 1936, the Reich Central Office for Combating the Gypsy Nuisance was set up. It took over the 19,000 files on 'Gypsies' from the Bavarian security police and began to classify and register them in order to make it easier for the police to persecute them in a systematic manner. Although 'Gypsies' were not specifically mentioned in the Nuremberg Laws of September 1935, they were considered to be 'racially alien' and therefore they were not allowed to marry or have sexual relations with 'Aryans'.

In 1936, Robert Ritter, a specialist in 'criminal biology', was appointed director of a new research unit on 'Gypsies': the Racial Hygiene and Population Biology Research Centre. Ritter's team included the anthropologists Adolf Würth, Gerhard Stein and Sophie Ehrhardt. Eva Justin, another of Ritter's researchers, received her doctorate in anthropology in 1943 for a dissertation on the subject of 'Gypsy' children. Ritter's investigators went around the cities and countryside collecting material on 'Gypsies'. As well as looking at official police files and municipal records, they photographed and interviewed 'Gypsies', and took head measurements and blood samples. Those 'Gypsies' who failed to cooperate were threatened with arrest and internment in a concentration camp.

Ritter argued that because they had come from India, the 'Gypsies' had originally been Aryans. He claimed that they had interbred with other races over the generations and over the course of their travels into and across Europe, so that the racial characteristics of the majority of the 'Gypsies' in Germany predisposed them to a criminal or 'asocial' lifestyle. Ritter believed that 90 per cent of Germany's 'Gypsies' were 'part-Gypsy'. Whilst he was prepared to allow the 'pure Gypsies' to pursue their lifestyle (although separately from the rest of the population), he called for the sterilisation and resettlement of the 'part-Gypsies', believing that they posed a genetic threat to the German 'national community'. Gerhard Stein claimed in 1936 that 'part-Gypsy bastards are generally dangerous hereditary criminals'.[9]

Ritter's research unit soon became part of Himmler's SS complex. On 16 July 1937, Himmler called for its findings to be evaluated by the Reich Central Office for Combating the Gypsy Nuisance.

On 8 December 1938, Himmler's circular on the 'Struggle against the Gypsy Nuisance' called for 'the racial affinity' of all 'Gypsies' to be established and distinctions to be made 'between pure and part-Gypsies in the final solution of the Gypsy question'.[10] He further called for the registration of all 'Gypsies' and 'vagrants living a Gypsy-like existence' with the police. He stated that:

> the treatment of the Gypsy question is part of the National Socialist task of national regeneration . . . the aim of measures taken by the State to defend the homogeneity of the German nation must be the physical separation of Gypsydom from the German nation, the prevention of miscegenation, and finally the regulation of the way of life of pure and part-Gypsies.[11]

This was another attempt to separate the 'Gypsies' from the rest of German society. They were to be issued with new identity cards: brown cards for 'pure Gypsies' and brown cards with a blue stripe for 'part-Gypsies'.

Throughout the 1930s, in addition to central state persecution, the 'Gypsies' were subject to measures on the part of individuals and local authorities to remove them and place them in ad hoc camps. The first of these separate 'Gypsy' camps was set up on the outskirts of Cologne. Plans for the establishment of a 'Gypsy' camp at Cologne had begun in May 1934. The Sinti and Roma were removed from their caravan plots and placed in a camp at Cologne-Bickendorf. An SS man occupied the guard hut at the entrance. From this point, he could see the entire camp, with the caravans arranged in two rows. A wire fence surrounded the camp. The 'Gypsies' had to report to the guard on leaving and entering the camp. Drastic and severe measures including police intimidation were employed to keep order. The Cologne Chief of Police noted: 'There is no fixed list of rules, they arise naturally.' Non-'Gypsies' were not allowed entry and the Gypsies were completely isolated from the local population. Frank Sparing shows that 'internment on the edge of town ensured that there was no longer any question of Gypsies who had been driven out returning to the town proper'.[12]

Following the Cologne model, municipal 'Gypsy' camps were set up on the outskirts of a number of other German cities, including Berlin, Dusseldorf, Essen and Frankfurt. These were established on the initiatives of local authorities or police forces, with no formal legal foundation. Their objective was to concentrate the entire 'Gypsy' population of a town or region in a single camp. The 'Gypsies' were then restricted in their movements, monitored and subjected to other constraints. These camps initially corralled the itinerant Roma, who corresponded most closely to the 'Gypsy' stereotype, and later interned 'Gypsies' who were more integrated into German society, when all 'Gypsies' were registered on racial grounds.

Sparing has argued: 'In contrast to measures undertaken during the Weimar Republic, which strove to sedentarise and assimilate the Gypsy population, this policy of concentration and isolation in separate internment camps represented a fundamental break with the past.'[13] Widespread anti-'Gypsy' sentiment and stereotypes were built upon and became central to National Socialist policy. As there was no central state initiative for the 'Gypsy' camps, the arrangements and the living conditions inside them varied greatly from town to town. Yet they did come to serve the larger aims of Nazi policy. The camps became reservoirs of forced labour and were the starting point for recording and classification by racial scientists. Furthermore, as Sybil Milton argues, after 1939 these camps evolved 'from municipal internment camps into assembly centres for systematic deportation to concentration camps, ghettos, and killing centres'.[14]

Shortly before the 1936 Olympics, the Berlin authorities rounded up some 600 'Gypsies' and dumped them on wasteland in Marzahn, a suburb north east of Berlin. The authorities justified this action on the grounds that they did not want the clean image of Berlin, the host city, to be sullied by the 'Gypsies'. Marzahn was subsequently ring-fenced and permanently guarded. The inmates of Marzahn received inadequate facilities, poor food and little medical attention. By 1939, the local authority was concerned about the possible spread of scarlet fever, diphtheria and tuberculosis from the camp to the population beyond its perimeters, and called for the physical restructuring and reclassification of Marzahn as a concentration camp, but this did not occur. Marzahn was a 'family' compound, where the internees were assembled and concentrated. Milton suggests that it also served 'as a transit depot for later deportations'. She further argues that Marzahn provided an example of the interagency cooperation between the police and public health officials, 'essential for subsequent developments resulting in the deportation and mass murder of German Gypsies'.

The German people's long-standing distrust and dislike of 'Gypsies' made it easier for the Nazi regime to implement its policies against them. The population was at worst hostile to and at best ambivalent towards the 'Gypsies'. The majority of the population took little interest in the plight of 'Gypsies'. Many were pleased that as undesirables, 'Gypsies' were kept away from them. They viewed the persecution of 'Gypsies' as a justified struggle against an antisocial and criminal element that did not fit into society. There was particular animosity and mistrust towards the Gypsies because of their perceived refusal to accept the norms of society. This apprehension was mutual – the German population mistrusted the 'Gypsies', and the 'Gypsies' mistrusted the German population. There was virtually no empathy or compassion among the German people towards 'Gypsy' victims of Nazi policy.

In some ways, the response of the 'Gypsies' to the Nazi persecution resembled that of the Jews. They had lived with oppression and discrimination for centuries, yet some considered Germany to be their home. Katja H., a German Sinti recalls: 'Like the Jews, we had homes there, businesses. We Sinti were upstanding Germans; we didn't think anything could happen to us. We were reared in Germany; it was our home. We thought of ourselves as Germans.'[15] However, many lived within the confines of their own culture groups and remained detached from mainstream society. As education was not considered of prime significance to the Roma, and as they moved about so much that they did not receive much schooling, most could not have read the decrees issued against them even if they had known about them. Alt and Folts point out that their illiteracy, together with their general suspicion of German society, 'effectively separated them from normal channels of communication'.[16] Whilst the Sinti and Roma, like the Jews, had been used to persecution and harassment, they too were not prepared for the unprecedented scale of a state policy of systematic genocide, nor did they anticipate it.

Himmler's perception and classification of the 'Gypsies' as an alien and inferior race in December 1938 provided a strong push for further policies against them. In September 1939, the removal of Germany's 'Gypsies' to Poland was proposed. In October 1939, Heydrich issued an order prohibiting all 'Gypsies' and 'part-Gypsies' not already in camps from changing their registered domiciles. Lewy points out that the escalation of anti-'Gypsy' measures after the outbreak of war was 'due to concerns about the alleged tendency of Gypsies to engage in espionage as well as pressure from local officials and the population at large to get rid of the Gypsy nuisance'.[17] In May 1940, 2,500 German 'Gypsies' were rounded up: 1,000 from Hamburg and Bremen; 1,000 from Cologne, Dusseldorf and Hanover; and 500 from Stuttgart and Frankfurt. Their property and possessions were confiscated and they were deported to Poland. The vast majority of the deported 'Gypsies' were forced into compulsory labour under SS control or into ghettoes in Poland.[18] Wanda G., a German Sinti, recalled the experience of her deportation:

We were unloaded from the transport . . . We were beaten with whips . . . We had to lie on the floor. We had no blankets, nothing. We were not allowed to take anything on the transport . . . We got no water. My mother gave us urine to drink.[19]

Plans to send all Germany's Sinti and Roma to the General Government region of Poland were not realised. The initial expulsion of 2,500 German 'Gypsies' in May 1940 was not followed by other deportations. The major obstacles were the jam created by the forced movement of over 300,000 Poles into the General Government region, as well as the objections by the General Governor, Hans Frank. There are also indications that Himmler was more concerned with other issues by the summer of 1940. A memorandum from Frank's office, dated 3 August 1940, stated that Himmler 'has ordered that the evacuation of Gypsies and part-Gypsies into the General Government is to be suspended until the general solution of the Jewish question'.[20] Therefore, further deportations of German 'Gypsies' did not follow at this time. Instead, Germany's 'Gypsies' had limitations placed upon their mobility and were subjected to an array of other restrictive and discriminatory measures. Many were forcibly sterilised, assigned to compulsory labour and dismissed from the armed services. More than ever, they were excluded from the 'national community' and treated as both social outcasts and racial aliens between 1940 and 1942.

## The *Porrajmos*: The Nazi Genocide of the Sinti and Roma

In the meantime, Nazi annihilation actions took on a genocidal character in the east. After Operation Barbarossa, the invasion of the Soviet Union on 22 June 1941, 'Gypsies' in the USSR became the victims of mass shootings by the *SS-Einsatzgruppen*. This marked the start of the systematic annihilation of the Sinti and Roma. They were killed on the grounds that they were 'racially inferior', or 'partisans', 'spies' and 'agents' for the enemies of National Socialism (for example, they were accused of being Judeo-Bolshevik informers). Michael Zimmermann points out that a greater number of 'Gypsies' were shot to death by the German Security Police and Order Police in the Soviet Union than were killed in the concentration camps and death camps. In the autumn of 1941 in German-occupied Serbia, the *Wehrmacht* took numerous male 'Gypsies' as 'hostages' and shot them to death in retaliation for the deaths of German soldiers and civilians. Furthermore, an estimated 36,000 Roma met their deaths in Transnistria during the war. In Hungary and Croatia too, tens of thousands of Roma were killed.[21]

In October 1942, Germany's remaining 'pure Gypsies' experienced a reprieve, initiated by Himmler, which incorporated some of Ritter's earlier ideas about 'pure Gypsies' being allowed to continue their lifestyle, but under careful guidelines that kept them separate from the German population. On 13 October 1942, a new regulation stated Himmler's intention that:

racially pure Gypsies be allowed a certain freedom of movement, so that they can itinerate in a fixed area, live according to their customs and mores, and follow an appropriate traditional occupation. The *Reichsführer-SS* [Himmler] assumes at the same time that the Gypsies encompassed by this order will conduct themselves irreproachably and not give rise to any complaints. Part-Gypsies, who from the point of view of the Gypsies are good part-Gypsies, shall be returned to specific racially pure Sinti Gypsy clans. If they apply for membership in a racially pure clan and the latter has no objections they shall be assigned the same status as racially pure Gypsies. The treatment of the remaining part-Gypsies and of the Rom-Gypsies is not affected by this intended new regulation.[22]

It is difficult to be sure of Himmler's reasons for this. He may have intended further racial research into the pure 'Gypsies', possibly later to include them in the stock of German blood if investigations confirmed their Aryan roots. He certainly promoted and facilitated the research of Georg Wagner on 'Gypsies' right up until 1945. In a letter of 3 December 1942, Martin Bormann, head of the Party Chancellery, complained to Himmler about the special arrangements for the racially pure 'Gypsies', suggesting that it would be unpopular with Hitler, as well as the lower ranks of the Party leadership and the population, to grant special privileges to any segment of the 'Gypsy' population. Despite ongoing objections and criticisms, Himmler's protection of Germany's 'pure Gypsies' continued and they were permitted to remain in Germany, albeit separated from the rest of the population.[23]

However, Himmler issued an order on 16 December 1942 that brought a new radicalisation to Nazi 'Gypsy' policy. The rest of Germany's 'Gypsies' were to be sent to Auschwitz. The procedures for this followed in an order of the RSHA (*Reichssicherheitshauptamt* or Reich Security Main Office), dated 29 January 1943. Zimmermann has pointed out that 'records in several cities show that the exception-provisions for "racially pure" Sinti and for "socially adapted gypsy half-castes" were not completely adhered to', and that the local criminal police frequently regarded the Auschwitz decree as 'an opportunity to make the area "gypsy free"'.[24] On 26 February 1943, the first transport of German 'Gypsies' arrived at the 'Gypsy camp' at Auschwitz-Birkenau (BIIe). The Sinti and Roma were deported to Auschwitz in families because the Nazi institutions involved with the persecution of Gypsies knew about their close family ties and decided that they needed to take this into account, according to Zimmermann, in order to 'keep the friction and resultant bureaucratic problems associated with the deportation and internment as small as possible'.[25]

Elisabeth Guttenberger, deported from Stuttgart in March 1943, recalls her arrival in Auschwitz: 'The first impression that we had of Auschwitz was terrible . . . It was awful. The people sat motionless in these bunks and just stared at us. I thought, I'm dreaming, I am in hell.'[26] Pollo R. describes his entry to Auschwitz:

> Longingly I looked at the gate which barred my way out of the compound filled with screaming humanity. Near me on several trucks were hundreds of nude men, women and children. Although they had not been on my transport, like me they were Gypsies, only they were from Silesia. I could hear and understand their prayers in Romany. They implored God (but in vain) to spare at least their children's lives. I was only fourteen at the time, and now realise that I had no real understanding of the situation that I was witnessing. But instinctively I knew that something unimaginable was going to happen. We were told to line up quickly. Those that lagged behind were hit with batons. One SS guard barked at us as he pointed to the chimney stacks which seemed to reach for the sky like long, threatening fingers, "This will be your way out of Auschwitz!"[27]

Unusually, BIIe was arranged as a family camp. (This was not the case in other Nazi camps where 'Gypsy' families, like those of other prisoners, were torn apart.) This allowed for a modicum of support and morale, as surviving family members lived in close proximity. The 'Gypsies' in the family camp attempted to maintain their language, customs and music, within the realms of what was possible. The camp consisted of thirty-two poorly constructed barracks, located in a swampy area. At first, it was not separated from the rest of the camp, but in July 1943, it was surrounded with an electric fence to separate it from other areas of Birkenau. Conditions in the 'Gypsy' camp were appalling. Rudolf Hoess, the Commandant of Auschwitz, acknowledged in his autobiography that 'if there had been any intention of keeping the "Gypsies" there for the duration of the war, the place lacked every kind of pre-condition to make this possible'. There were major outbreaks of typhus, smallpox and other diseases.

A disease called noma rotted the skin and left large holes in the cheeks of 'Gypsy' children. There was almost no medical treatment available. The Sinti and Roma at BIIe died in thousands from disease, exposure and starvation.

Furthermore, the 'Gypsies' at Auschwitz were subjected to medical experimentation. Josef Mengele undertook experiments on 'Gypsy' twins for Otmar von Verschuer, the Director of the Kaiser Wilhelm Institute for Anthropology in Berlin. Mengele conducted one project on 'eye colour' and another on 'specific protein bodies'. The victims of the medical experiments were subsequently gassed, shot or killed by lethal injection. From April 1944, those 'Gypsies' capable of working or still required for medical experiments were relocated to Buchenwald, Ravensbrück and Flossenbürg. They left behind 2,897 people – the women and children, the aged and those unable to work. In August 1944, the camp was liquidated and those left behind were gassed to death and cremated in a single action known as *Zigeunernacht* ('Gypsy night'). Filip Müller, assigned to the task of burning corpses, was an eyewitness to *Zigeunernacht*:

Towards midnight, the changing room was full of people. The disorder grew from minute to minute. From all sides there were desperate cries, wailing and cursing accusations to be heard. Chanting got loud. "We are German citizens. We have committed no crime." . . . As they made their last journey many wept in despair . . . For some time we could still hear despairing screams and cries from the gas chambers until the deadly gas had carried out its work and brought the last voice to suffocation.[28]

In October 1944, 218 'Gypsy' women and 800 'Gypsy' children were transported back to Auschwitz from Buchenwald and killed in Crematorium V. In all, some 20,078 Sinti and Roma were killed at Auschwitz – thirty-two were shot after trying to escape, 6,432 were gassed and 13,614 died as a result of the conditions in the camp.[29]

Apart from Auschwitz, the Sinti and Roma were interned in many other Nazi camps. Daily existence in the camps and chances for survival depended upon a number of factors: the particular camp they were in, the need for their forced labour, the character and caprices of their captors, luck and their own survival skills. Day-to-day existence was a continual struggle for survival – against hunger, cold, beatings, compulsory physical labour, dirt and disease. The daily struggle for sustenance is pre-eminent among survivor recollections. The prisoners received wholly inadequate rations of food that was often, in any case, inedible. They tried to obtain food for themselves or their loved ones using any possible method – including, for those assigned to work in kitchen areas, stealing and smuggling leftover scraps. Asta F. worked extra shifts in the Ravensbrück kitchen. She recalls:

> The food we were provided with was nothing – soup without any base, just water with whatever was available thrown in. Some lard or grease, cabbage and potatoes, if we could get them. But not enough of anything solid or nourishing to chew on. But we had salt and it was hot. There was usually some kind of bread, many times hard as a rock, many times covered with blue spots of mould, but we dipped in. We survived.[30]

Forced labour on the meagre rations meant that many prisoners could not survive. The prisoners fought against disease and many died of smallpox, dysentery, scarlet fever, spotted fever, typhoid and tuberculosis in the concentration camps. Furthermore, they were worked to death through hard labour. Others died during the protracted roll calls where they had to stand for many hours in freezing temperatures. In addition to these daily trials, the 'Gypsy' prisoners were subjected to medical experimentation, as well as being beaten and tortured. SS doctors carried out lethal medical experiments on the 'Gypsies' at Dachau, Natzweiler, Sachsenhausen, Buchenwald and Ravensbrück. For example, at Dachau, 'Gypsy' inmates were used in experiments to establish how much salt water a person could drink before dying. At Ravensbrück, many 'Gypsy' women were subjected to barbarous experiments on sterilisation without anaesthetics. At Buchenwald, 'Gypsy' prisoners were subjected to typhus fever, cold shock and other experiments. Alt and Folts show that 'repeated brutality by the guards and Kapos severely complicated life for the Gypsies'.[31] Eugen Kogon recalled the fate of a 'Gypsy' inmate at Buchenwald who attempted to escape in 1938:

Commandant Koch had him placed in a wooden box, one side covered by chicken wire. The box was only large enough to permit the prisoner to crouch. Koch then had large nails driven through the boards, piercing the victim's flesh at the slightest movement. The Gypsy was exhibited to the whole camp in this cage. He was kept in the roll call area for two days and three nights without food. His dreadful screams had long lost any semblance of humanity. On the morning of the third day he was finally relieved of his suffering by an injection of poison.[32]

# Conclusion

It is difficult to be precise about the total number of Sinti and Roma who were murdered by the Nazis and their collaborators during the course of the Second World War. Estimates of the number who perished in the *Porrajmos* vary from 250,000 to over 1 million. This imprecision is partly because of the inaccurate and scant records of Roma and Sinti populations in Europe before the Second World War, partly because of the haphazard methods used to capture and kill the 'Gypsies,' and because 'Gypsy' prisoners were not a high priority to the Nazis. Few accurate records were kept of their deaths. As Ulrich König has argued:

> The count of half a million Sinti and Roma murdered between 1939 and 1945 is too low to be tenable; for example in the Soviet Union many of the Romani dead were listed under non-specific labels such as "remaining to be liquidated", "hangers-on" and "partisans" . . . The final number of the dead Sinti and Roma may never be determined.[33]

Furthermore, many of the massacres of 'Gypsies' in Eastern and Southern Europe, which occurred at numerous sites, were not recorded, as they took place in fields and forests. In addition, most 'Gypsy' families were killed in their entirety, leaving no survivors to detail the number of dead. In the next chapter, we shall move to the post-war period and to the Asian continent to examine events in Cambodia between 1975 and 1979.

# Questions for Further Discussion

1 Why were the Sinti and Roma forgotten victims of National Socialism for so long?

2 In what ways were Nazi anti-'Gypsy' attitudes and policies similar to or distinctive from earlier anti-'Gypsy' attitudes and policies?

3 On what grounds did the Nazi regime exclude the Sinti and Roma from German society?

4 Why did Himmler make a distinction between 'pure Gypsies' and 'part-Gypsies'?

5 When and why did the Nazi government decide to annihilate the Sinti and Roma?

# Further Reading

Alt, B. and Folts, S., *Weeping Violins: The Gypsy Tragedy In Europe* (Kirksville, MO, 1996).

Burleigh, M. and Wippermann, W., *The Racial State: Germany 1933–1945* (Cambridge, 1991).

Fings, K., Heuss, H. and Sparing, F., *From 'Race Science' to the Camps: The Gypsies during the Second World War* (Hatfield, 1997).

Hancock, I., *The Pariah Syndrome: An Account of Gypsy Slavery and Persecution* (Ann Arbor, MI, 1987).

Hancock, I., 'Romanies and the Holocaust', in D. Stone (ed.), *The Historiography of the Holocaust* (Basingstoke, 2004), pp. 383–96.

Kenrick, D. (ed.), *The Gypsies during the Second World War: The Final Chapter* (Hatfield, 2006).

Kenrick, D. and Puxon, G., *The Destiny of Europe's Gypsies* (London, 1972).

Kenrick, D. and Puxon, G., *Gypsies under the Swastika* (Hatfield, 2009).

Lewy, G., 'Himmler and the "Racially Pure Gypsies"', *Journal of Contemporary History* Vol. 34, No. 2 (1999), pp. 201–14.

Lewy, G., *The Nazi Persecution of the Gypsies* (Oxford, 2000).

Margalit, G., *Germany and its Gypsies* (Madison, WI, 2002).

Milton, S., '"Gypsies" as Social Outsiders in Nazi Germany', in R. Gellately and N. Stoltzfus (eds), *Social Outsiders in Nazi Germany* (Princeton, NJ, 2001).

Schulze, R. (ed.), *The Holocaust in History and Memory. The Porrajmos: The 'Gypsy Holocaust' and the Continuing Discrimination of Roma and Sinti after 1945*, Vol. 3 (2010).

Weiss-Wendt, A. (ed.), *The Nazi Genocide of the Roma: Reassessment and Commemoration* (New York and Oxford, 2013).

# 5

# Cambodia: Genocide or Politicide?

The Khmer Rouge (Cambodian Communist Party), led by Pol Pot, ruled Cambodia from April 1975 to January 1979. The date 17 April 1975 signified Day One of Year Zero in the new revolutionary calendar of the Khmer Rouge. The Khmer Rouge leadership undertook a project of social engineering to create a completely new Cambodian society, which was classless, moneyless and based upon a collectivised agrarian economy. The Khmer Rouge sealed off Cambodia from the outside world, expelling foreign embassies and press agencies, closing down media outlets and restricting communications drastically inside the country. Nostalgic for a glorious Cambodian past and inspired by fanatical irredentism, the Khmer Rouge aimed to recreate the lost grandeur of the medieval Khmer empire – centred around the temple of Angkor Wat – and to reconstruct its power, taking back lost territory from Thailand and Vietnam. The Khmer Rouge employed systematic terror and violence to establish and consolidate its new, revolutionary regime in Cambodia. The use of terror and the creation of a climate of fear were designed to create a homogeneous society and to destroy any potential resistance or dissent.

Pol Pot (born Saloth Sar) led his communist party to victory in 1975, after five years of civil war, due to a number of factors. Among the most important was the role played by the USA in the economic and military destabilisation of Cambodia as a consequence of the Vietnam War. American bombardment of the Cambodian countryside provided recruitment propaganda for Pol Pot's communist party and won many peasants to his cause. However, once in power, the Khmer Rouge enacted policies that resulted in the death of vast numbers of Cambodians, through execution, starvation and exhaustion. Pol Pot's communist revolution engendered a death toll of between 1.7 million and 2 million Cambodians, out of an estimated total population in Cambodia of 8 million before the revolution. Hence, the Khmer Rouge regime brought about the death of nearly one-quarter of the country's population. The nature of these mass killings has produced a significant debate among experts in the field, between those who argue that it was indeed a case of genocide and those who maintain that it was not. This chapter explores some of the key arguments by scholars surrounding whether the mass killings were genocide or politicide. As the name suggests, politicide means the killing of political opponents. Whilst most scholars concur that the events in Cambodia were genocidal, some have argued that they were politicidal. Critical academic debates in relation to Cambodia not only have provided a better understanding of how this mass murder unfolded, but also have contributed to the broader discourse of genocide studies.

# Debates

Manus Midlarsky has distinguished the mass murders in Cambodia under Pol Pot as politicide rather than genocide. He argues that 'in fact genocidal activity was only a small proportion of the killing and that the vast majority of Cambodians died in a politicide'.[1] He contends that the state killings in Cambodia could be attributed to communist ideology and demonstrates their close affinity with similar actions in the USSR and China. Midlarsky conceptualises 'an arc of Communist politicide . . . from the Soviet Union to China and on to Cambodia'.[2] For example, it is estimated that 'at least 45 million people died unnecessarily between 1958 and 1962' in China under Mao.[3] Similarly to China in the 1950s, Cambodia in 1975 had great aspirations for hasty industrialisation and collectivisation, in line with communist ideology. In order to achieve this goal quickly and simultaneously to keep control over the population, collectivisation was introduced. Pol Pot believed that Cambodia needed to make progress very swiftly.

Khmer Rouge policy meant that Cambodian peasants would no longer have their own plots, but that everything was to be organised collectively. In addition, communal living was introduced, such as common dining rooms and facilities for looking after children. The systematic relocation of Cambodians and the way of life on the communes closely imitated the Chinese Great Leap Forward. Indeed, Pol Pot spoke of his own Super Great Leap Forward in Cambodia, centred on self-sufficiency.[4]

In addition, Pol Pot emulated the Cultural Revolution in China under Mao Zedong. Indeed, Pol Pot visited China in 1966 at the height of the Cultural Revolution. A number of characteristics of Mao's Cultural Revolution in China were repeated in Cambodia in the following decade. The first similarity was in the emphasis on youth and its crucial role in the revolution. The Chinese Red Guards, who pushed through Mao's Cultural Revolution, were almost all late teenagers, young adults and students. Mao preferred them to the 'tainted' and especially Westernised older people, often from urban areas, who were not to be trusted. In Cambodia, the Khmer Rouge too considered purity only to be found in the young. The Khmer Rouge regarded them to be untainted elements. Another characteristic found both in the Chinese Cultural Revolution and the situation in Cambodia under the Khmer Rouge was the attack on vested interests. In China, the Cultural Revolution had targeted party cadres, officials and peasants with an economic stake in the status quo or rich peasants (similar to the kulak class in the USSR). The Khmer Rouge in Cambodia implemented similar practices.

The core of the politicide lay in the primacy of politics in the revolutions of both the Chinese Communist Party and the Khmer Rouge. Both Mao and Pol Pot believed that the intellectuals stood in the way of the revolution. They determined that those with expertise, who emerged as a leadership class with its own concerns, opposed the aims of the revolution. In their place, Mao and Pol Pot used young people with political zeal and correct revolutionary attitudes. Straight after seizing power, Pol Pot removed urban populations directly to rural areas so that they could not damage the revolution. Many died from exhaustion, starvation, disease and malnutrition; many others were executed. Pol Pot wanted to ensure that no urban or Westernised elites were present in the new administration. This entailed a swift emptying out of the cities. The Khmer Rouge emulated the anti-urban and anti-Western attitude of the Chinese Communist Party. In order to reduce the possibility of failure, the Khmer Rouge emptied the cities completely and used an unprecedented scale of violence to achieve its aims.

An even earlier model for the Khmer Rouge can be found in the death toll of Stalin's collectivisation efforts between 1929 and 1933. Here an estimated 6–7 million deaths mainly through famine occurred. In addition, the landowning class of peasants, the kulaks, who opposed the collectivisation policies were summarily shot or deported to distant and inhospitable regions. Robert Conquest has estimated 6.5 million deaths in the dekulakisation process in the USSR.[5] Moreover, similarly to Stalin, Pol Pot also purged both the party and Khmer society due to fears for his own position. Members of the party organisation, the military and others were executed as state enemies. Midlarsky concludes that the '20 per cent victimisation rate in Cambodia is much more in keeping with the scripted mass murders initiated by Stalin and Mao' than with the Nazi genocide of the Jews, the Turkish genocide of the Armenians or the Hutu genocide of the Tutsi, in which, in all of these cases the victimisation rates of genocide 'ranged between 66 and 70 per cent'.[6]

The nature of the Khmer Rouge regime has generated a variety of interpretations among experts in this field. David Chandler maintains that the Khmer Rouge leadership did not intend to utilise its revolution as a means to destroy particular ethnic groups, and that the deaths in Cambodia during the Khmer Rouge era were the unintended consequence of a social revolution.[7] Chandler also contends that 'the regime discriminated against enemies of the revolution rather than against specific ethnic or religious groups'.[8] Michael Vickery points to 'very long roots in Cambodia' of 'patterns of extreme violence'.[9] He further argues that the Khmer Rouge era was characterised by the revolutionary terror of the peasants against the city dwellers, intellectuals and professional classes, and that the Khmer Rouge regime was 'a victorious peasant revolution, perhaps the first real one in modern times'.[10] He contends that the Khmer Rouge leadership was 'pulled along' by the peasant class, rather than being influenced by external communist models, such as Stalinism.[11] Samir Amin concurs that this was principally a peasant revolution. Serge Thion argues that the Khmer Rouge regime was 'a bloody mess', characterised by factionalism and regional differences.[12] Ben Kiernan, by contrast, has suggested that the Khmer Rouge leadership achieved 'successful top-down domination' and 'unprecedented' power in Cambodia.[13] Anthony Barnett also asserts the case for a highly centralised, authoritarian regime.[14]

# The Khmer Rouge and its Policies

After winning the Cambodian Civil War (1970–5), the Khmer Rouge executed former soldiers, officials and policemen of the defeated Lon Nol government. They usually killed their entire families as well. An eyewitness, who was a former army member, recalled the scene as he and his family were taken to be executed:

> The Khmer Rouge were stuffing the mouths of those they were leading with rags and grass to prevent them from screaming and were cutting their throats like animals – the throats of men, women, old folk and children alike. I managed to escape.[15]

The new regime targeted the city people, relocated them to the countryside and labelled them as 'new people'. This policy was directed at all civilians who did not live in the areas 'liberated' by the Khmer Rouge during the civil war. Since they had lived in the 'enemy zone' during the civil war, the Khmer Rouge questioned their loyalty. The Khmer Rouge regarded these people as impure and therefore expendable, and venerated a peasant lifestyle in contrast to what they regarded as the decadence of the cities. The regime forced nearly 2 million people out of the capital city alone, Phnom Penh, even emptying out the hospitals. Any resisters to the 'evacuation' policy were killed on the spot. In the following weeks, Cambodia's other cities were evacuated. The regime justified the evacuation of the cities on the grounds of the threat of American bombing and the difficulties in supplying food to the cities. But in reality, this was a tool to counter the threat of any possible resistance to the new Khmer Rouge government or a counter-revolution against it. The abandonment of the cities severed city dwellers from their cultural, social and economic milieus. The existence of established checkpoints along the routes out of the cities indicates that the emptying out of the urban areas was planned and implemented to achieve specific policy aims, rather than for any other reason. Deaths along the evacuation routes out of the cities resulted from heat, lack of sustenance and the lack of any medical provision. The aged and infirm fared the worst. The Khmer Rouge viewed the cities as corrupt, decadent and full of Western influences. The regime forcibly removed former city dwellers – the 'new people' – from their homes. The Khmer Rouge cadres directed their compulsory work on a variety of public works schemes. They constructed dams, irrigation dykes and villages in malarial zones. Many died in these areas under harsh conditions of labour. They were considered to have led corrupt lives and therefore needed to be trained to be productive workers. They lost all their former status to become the lowest level in the new hierarchy of Cambodian society. They were meted out the hardest labour and forced to work the longest hours. A Khmer Rouge cadre explained the emptying out of the cities thus:

> From now on if the people want to eat, they should go out and work in the rice paddies. They should learn lives depend on a grain of rice. Ploughing the soil, planting and harvesting rice will teach them the real value of things. Cities are evil.[16]

Kiernan argues that the Khmer Rouge imposed conditions upon the 'new people' as a whole group that were designed to bring about their eventual destruction. The regime specifically targeted doctors, teachers, lawyers, intellectuals and civil servants. A Western education marked out these groups for destruction, in line with the anti-Western ideology of the regime. This type of purification campaign was repeated to eliminate any perceived 'enemies' of the revolution and the regime.

Certainly, the communist revolution in Cambodia was intended to be speedier than that in either China or the USSR. Benjamin Valentino notes that the Khmer Rouge 'consciously set out to surpass China and the Soviet Union in the speed and scope with which they implemented communism'.[17] Pol Pot's aim was to rapidly transform the Cambodian countryside from small peasant plots, which were privately owned, to large-scale, state-owned collectivised farms. Pol Pot believed that collectivisation would modernise and rationalise the country's agricultural system. Instead of subsistence farming, he envisioned the production of vast quantities of rice, which could be used to feed the army or exported in return for capital to develop Cambodia's industry. In agricultural terms, the Khmer Rouge aimed at trebling the harvest to 3 tons or more per hectare. Collectivisation, however, also had a political purpose. Pol Pot considered that this policy could be used to control segments of the population that were opposed to his regime and to eradicate old beliefs and customs. In addition, it was hoped that the benefits of collectivisation, in particular an increase in living standards, would win popular support for the Khmer Rouge. Furthermore, the new socialist order was based upon complete acceptance of the regime and the subjugation of the individual to the state and its demands.

Pol Pot made no attempt to introduce his new system of collectivisation gradually. On the contrary, he called for alacrity. He criticised other communist states that failed to eradicate private property completely and called for an entirely collectivised system. All vestiges of capitalism were to be eradicated. Even small private vegetable patches were disallowed. Pol Pot was willing to use violence to quell opposition or potential resistance. He introduced countrywide collectivisation in 1976, unwilling to delay its implementation. He addressed his fellow party members, stating:

> Why must we move so swiftly? Because enemies attack and torment us. From the east and the west they persist in pounding and worrying us . . . There is no time to wait for another occasion; waiting until 1977 . . . would be very slow. We won't wait. We must do it even though we have only just emerged from war.

Total collectivisation was achieved within two years. This was a very fast-paced revolution.

Furthermore, as well as being units of economic production, the collective farms were used to control the population and to build a communist society. The political socialisation of the masses took place. The Khmer Rouge instilled its ideology into children from an early age. Children were regarded as the 'blank slates' of the revolution. They were encouraged to spy on their older family members and report behaviour or conversations that did not conform to Khmer Rouge ideology. The regime removed children from their parents to diminish family bonds and to replace them with loyalty to the Khmer Rouge instead. It disseminated propaganda and controlled all aspects of life. It encouraged communal eating in order to promote loyalty to the regime. Language, hairstyle and clothing came under strict scrutiny. The Khmer Rouge even controlled marriages, as love was deemed to be selfish and the needs of the regime were to take precedence over individual affairs of the heart. Political education controlled what people could and could not do and was a manifestation of Khmer Rouge power. The regime used starvation, forced labour and long, arduous hours to control the Cambodian people and to re-educate them when necessary.

National homogeneity was one of the main aims of the Khmer Rouge. The regime maintained that there should henceforth be one single nation and one single language, the Khmer language. The Khmer Rouge suppressed the languages and cultures of the various ethnic groups and nationalities that had lived in Cambodia for many centuries. Ethnic groups that were deemed to be hostile to the revolution and incapable of being re-educated were eradicated. The Khmer Rouge slogan 'it isn't enough to cut down a bad plant, it must be uprooted' meant that certain sectors of the Cambodian population were to be removed in their entirety.

## Mass Murder

The systematic massacre of ethnic and religious groups by the Khmer Rouge leadership can be characterised as genocide (instead of politicide), although not all scholars concur on this point. The Khmer Rouge wanted to wipe out religion from Cambodia and persecuted the most dominant religious groups. It selected Buddhist monks and Muslim clerics, in particular, for annihilation. Ben Kiernan estimates that by January 1979, fewer than 2,000 of Cambodia's 70,000 monks had survived.[18] Chanthou Boua notes, 'Buddhism was eradicated from the face of the country in just one year'.[19] The Khmer Rouge also targeted ethnic and nationality groups such as the Chams, Chinese,

Vietnamese and other foreigners. In 1975, the Khmer Rouge banned by decree the existence of ethnic Vietnamese, Chinese and Chams, as well as twenty other minority groups. It slaughtered the entire Vietnamese population of Cambodia, ordering them to leave and then killing them on their way to Vietnam as they fled from Cambodia. It considered Cambodia's ethnic Vietnamese minority to be an internal threat to the survival of the state. The Khmer Rouge also killed more than half of the Chinese population of Cambodia. By 1979, only 200,000 out of a pre-revolutionary population of 425,000 Chinese had survived the Pol Pot regime.[20] Kiernan argues that the Chinese were targeted because they lived mainly in urban areas, and the revolution aimed to eradicate city dwellers. Hence, they were categorised as enemies primarily because of their urban way of life, although they were also outlawed as an ethnic group. The Chinese language was banned and the Khmer Rouge wanted to eradicate the Chinese community. The Chinese were exposed to conditions of hunger and disease that were intended to prevent their survival as an ethnic group.

Moreover, the Khmer Rouge targeted the Chams on account of their Muslim religion, language, culture and autonomy. The Chams were perceived as a threat to the intentions of the new, secular Cambodian society envisaged by the Khmer Rouge. The Khmer Rouge destroyed their religious texts, closed down their schools, banned the Cham language and prevented women from wearing sarongs and dressing their hair in their traditional style. They forced them to eat pork and to raise pigs, obliging them to act against their religious beliefs. Those who tried to resist these demands were killed. The ethnic Chams faced systematic state persecution on grounds of their religion. By January 1979, 100,000 out of 250,000 Chams had perished at the hands of the Khmer Rouge regime.[21] Only twenty of their community leaders out of 113 survived the Pol Pot years. Furthermore, the Khmer Rouge reduced the Thai minority population from 20,000 to 8,000 and the Lao ethnic minority population was reduced by nearly half, from 1,800 families to 800 families. The entire Kola group of 2,000 members was wiped out during the Khmer Rouge era.[22] In such cases, in which an entire ethnic or religious group was deliberately eliminated, the case for genocide is certainly valid.

The Pol Pot regime resettled and eradicated the Cambodian population that lived in the Eastern Zone (see Map 5), which bordered

**MAP 5** *Cambodia.*

Vietnam. The Eastern Zone was initially an exceptional territory of the country, in which 1.7 million Buddhists had a relatively autonomous way of life. Economically, this territory was significant because of its rice fields and rubber plantations. Strategically, it was important because of the state boundary with Vietnam. Furthermore, in a revolutionary society, in which the Khmer Rouge leadership wanted to achieve homogeneity, the relative independence of this area was not sustainable.

In May 1978, Pol Pot sent his most loyal southwestern troops to the Eastern Zone to bring it into line with the rest of the Cambodian state and to 'purify' it. The policy of 'purification' meant the mass murder of the people living there, as well as the deportation of tens of thousands of its inhabitants to the Northwestern Zone. They were given blue scarves (kromar) to mark them out as 'impure' and dissident. The policy of distinguishing a group in this way was markedly similar to the Nazi policy of forcing Jews to wear the Yellow Star that we noted in Chapter 3.

Pol Pot called for the party cadres to eliminate 'traitors', 'enemies' and 'ugly microbes'.[23] The terminology here is significant, as it legitimised and endorsed mass murder. Conceptualised as 'microbes', the enemy was not only dehumanised, but also specifically and directly equated with bacteria that needed to be eradicated. The Khmer Rouge dealt with its enemies by means of torture, beatings and executions. Victims were removed from their homes in the dead of night. The next day they had simply disappeared and no one asked questions, as it was too dangerous to do so (see Figure 5).

In addition, there were numerous wholesale massacres, such as the Tonle Sap Massacre in December 1977. Ronnie Yismut, the one remaining survivor out of a group of seventy-nine victims, recalled in his testimony:

They took us south through a familiar muddy road towards the lake, which was about six or seven miles away . . . There were only five of them. They couldn't possibly kill all 79 of us – could they? . . . If we didn't die of starvation, exhaustion, or mosquito bites, there was a good chance that we might be killed by the hands of the soldiers. The thought of me actually coming face to face with death now terrified me . . . A soldier walked towards me, yanking away a cotton towel and shredding it into small strips. I was the first one to be tied up tightly by the soldiers with one of the strips. I was stunned and quite terrified. I began to resist a little. After a few blows to the head with rifle butts, I could only let them do as they pleased with me. My head began to bleed from a wound. I was still semi-conscious – I could feel the pain and blood flowing down on my face.

Having been subsequently rendered unconscious from being beaten, he woke up the next morning to see:

**FIGURE 5** *Skulls at Choeung Ek, Cambodia.*

the scattered bodies laying in every direction. Some of them were beyond recognition. Some were completely stripped naked . . . I began to fade and feel as though my life was slipping away. I passed out again on top of the dead bodies. I was totally out cold.[24]

Cannibalism occurred too – not as a common or typical characteristic of the regime's brutality, but nevertheless significant enough to be mentioned here. Khmer Rouge cadres were at liberty to cannibalise their victims because the policies of the regime gave them carte blanche to do with their victims as they wished. The slicing open of the abdomen and removal of the liver to eat was one of these types of excesses. Similarly to rape and torture, cannibalism violated the most essential integrity of the victim's body. As Eric Weitz has noted, cannibalism represented 'the utter, complete degradation of the individual, the utter domination of another through the decimation and consumption of the body. As an act of total power, nothing could be more complete than this.'[25] Furthermore, cannibalism instilled fear among other potential victims. Terrified survivors who witnessed such scenes heard the party cadres discussing their cannibalistic deeds with the intention of being heard. They did this both in order to engender fear and to heighten their own sense of power and superiority.

Forced labour, the purges of 'enemies' and mass executions characterised the Pol Pot regime. As Weitz has described, violence was 'an intrinsic element of the Khmer Rouge view of the state'.[26] An estimated 14,000 political victims of Khmer Rouge purges were killed at the notorious site of Tuol Sleng (or S–21) alone.[27] This exemplified the nationwide and systematic terror meted out through incarceration, interrogation, torture and execution implemented by the Khmer Rouge. These brutal measures were accompanied by the vast death toll from starvation and exhaustion. Khmer Rouge purges reached a peak in the last two years of the regime (1977 and 1978), with the mass slaughter of hundreds of thousands of people. For example, a major purge took place in the Northwestern Zone in 1977–8.

When Vietnam and Laos signed a treaty of cooperation in July 1977, Cambodia found itself potentially surrounded by hostile forces. The relationship between Cambodia and Vietnam deteriorated very quickly after that. Cambodian forces made repeated incursions into Vietnamese territory. In response to the refusal of the Khmer Rouge to negotiate, Vietnamese troops invaded in late 1977, and conflict continued throughout the following year. Midlarsky notes that as a result of Vietnamese incursions, 'even non-Vietnamese residents of the East closest to Vietnam would be subject to Khmer Rouge butchery'.[28] The final months before the Vietnamese invasion were the most brutal, in particular, in the Eastern Zone with the purge that began in May 1978. In December 1978, the Vietnamese mounted a major offensive that brought down the Khmer Rouge in January 1979. A group of Cambodian military officers, in alliance with the Vietnamese, succeeded in overthrowing the Pol Pot regime in January 1979. The era of the killing fields came to an end.

# Conclusion

The Khmer Rouge regime had mercilessly targeted and massacred a very significant proportion of Cambodia's population in the name of its communist revolution. The victims of the Khmer Rouge were ethnically and religiously motivated in many cases. In particular, the eradication of the Buddhist monks and the Chams on grounds of their religion and the Vietnamese and the Chinese on grounds of their ethnicity is illustrative of this. In other cases, policies directed against urban people, intellectuals or 'enemies' of the regime were largely politically motivated. The political purges of enemies of the regime were similar to those of Stalin's Great Terror in the 1930s and Mao's Cultural Revolution in the 1960s. In this respect, they were attempts by Pol Pot to protect the revolution from its enemies. The killings in Cambodia were directed not only at specific individuals, but at their whole families as well. The anthropologist Alexander Hinton suggests that the regime's resolution to wipe out entire families was based upon the traditional Cambodian cultural 'model of disproportionate revenge', so that by destroying the family line of an individual, the potential for future vengeance was removed.[29] The Khmer Rouge leadership utilised this aspect of Cambodian culture to encourage its cadres to settle 'class grudges'. The mass killings were also a reflection of Pol Pot's obsession with disloyalty and perceived enemies.

In the final analysis, all of the victims of the regime were murdered because they were considered to be undesirable or impure. Kiernan contends that the Khmer Rouge was able 'to plan such mass murders precisely because of its concentrated power . . . The regime's intent was clear and was successful.'[30] Steven Ratner and Jason Abrams concur: 'the existing literature presents a strong *prima facie* case that the Khmer Rouge committed acts of genocide against the Cham minority group, the ethnic Vietnamese, Chinese, and Thai minority groups, and the Buddhist monkhood.'[31] Mass gravesites across the country testify to the wholesale massacres of both ethnic and religious groups and political enemies. The revolutionary ideology of the Khmer Rouge resulted in the annihilation of an estimated one-quarter of the population of Cambodia between 1975 and 1979. In the next chapter, we move to Europe in the 1990s, to examine the bloody conflicts in the former Yugoslavia, which brought the subject of genocide into sharper focus in academic discourse and popular consciousness.

# Questions for Further Discussion

1   What is the difference between the terms genocide and politicide?

2   Are the Cambodian 'killing fields' better understood as the outcome of genocide or politicide?

3   Why is there so much disagreement among scholars about the nature of the Pol Pot regime?

4   What were the commonalities and differences between Pol Pot's regime in Cambodia and those of Stalin in the USSR and Mao Zedong in China?

5   Which ethnic and religious groups did the Khmer Rouge target for persecution and annihilation, and why?

# Further Reading

Chandler, D., *The Tragedy of Cambodian History: Politics, War and Revolution since 1945* (New Haven, CT and London, 1991).

Chandler, D., *Brother Number One: A Political Biography of Pol Pot* (Boulder, CO, 1999).

Cruvellier, T., *The Master of Confessions: The Making of a Khmer Rouge Torturer* (New York, 2014).

Him, C., *When Broken Glass Floats: Growing Up under the Khmer Rouge* (New York, 2000).

Hinton, A., *Why Did They Kill? Cambodia in the Shadow of Genocide* (Berkeley, CA, 2005).

Kiernan, B., *The Pol Pot Regime: Race, Power, and Genocide in Cambodia under the Khmer Rouge, 1975–1979* (New Haven, CT and London, 2008).

Kissi, E., 'Genocide in Cambodia and Ethiopia', in R. Gellately and B. Kiernan (eds), *The Specter of Genocide: Mass Murder in Historical Perspective* (Cambridge, 2003), pp. 307–23.

Short, P., *Pol Pot: Anatomy of a Nightmare* (New York, 2006).

Ung, L., *First They Killed My Father: A Daughter of Cambodia Remembers* (New York, 2000).

Vickery, M., *Cambodia 1975–1982* (Boston, MA, 1984).

region have concurred that it was not ancient hatred that caused the conflicts and genocide of the 1990s. For example, Norman Cigar shows that 'all three communities in Bosnia-Herzegovina lived for centuries in relative harmony'.[2] The capacity for ethnic co-existence before the 1990s is further illustrated by the high rates of intermarriages among Serbs, Muslims and Croatians during the Tito regime.

Another contributing element to a tense situation was growing economic instability. Unemployment grew and economic productivity declined during the 1980s as a result of a combination of factors including mismanagement and technical obsolescence in many industries. In addition, the new developments towards state-building created a momentum of their own, as previously the borders of the republics in the federation had never had to satisfy the needs of independent states. As Susan Woodward notes: 'Once nationalists turned to state-building, there was an additional reason on many sides for contesting existing republican borders.'[3] Manus Midlarsky adds to this assessment, writing that 'ethnic cleansing, and its genocidal corollary, had its roots in a democratization process associated with the emergence of sovereignty in the new post-Cold War period'.[4] As the new states were formed, ethnic cleansing became the chief method used to bring about homogeneity in the ethno-religious identity of their residents. Radicalisation certainly drew on earlier tensions.

Much of the debate surrounding the mass atrocities in the former Yugoslavia has centred upon whether or not they amounted to genocide. Both the International Criminal Tribunal for the Former Yugoslavia (ICTY) and the International Court of Justice (ICJ) accorded that the mass executions at Srebrenica constituted genocide, because specific intent to destroy a group in whole or in part fitted with the legal definition of genocide. However, the ICJ ruled that other crimes committed during the conflict in Bosnia did not meet this legal definition. William Schabas, a leading expert in international law and genocide scholar, notes: 'This debate is not about whether the crimes . . . actually took place; it is only about whether they are most properly described as crimes against humanity, rather than "genocide"'.[5] A similar argument can be applied to the events in Kosovo later in the decade, and there remains dispute among scholars about whether or not the case in Kosovo can be termed genocide. We shall return to this question later in the chapter.

## Historical Context

The Balkan region had experienced a turbulent history. During the eighteenth century, the Austrian Empire regained lands from the Turks and drove out Muslim inhabitants from Hungary and Dalmatia. In the nineteenth century, the new states of Serbia, Greece and Montenegro emerged. They also expelled former Muslim rulers from their land. The Balkan Wars at the beginning of the twentieth century saw new massacres of civilians. The Carnegie Commission reported in 1914: 'The burning of villages and the exodus of the defeated population is a normal and traditional event in all Balkan wars and insurrections.' The worst massacres occurred during the Second World War.[6] In Croatia, the Ustasha, led by Ante Pavelić, the *Poglavnik* (supreme leader), and allied to Nazi Germany, aimed to annihilate Serbian populations. They killed the Serbians not only for being partisans, but also for being Serbian. Between 1941 and 1945 some 80,000 prisoners – the majority of whom were Serbs, but also Jews and Roma – perished at Jasenovac, the largest concentration camp in Yugoslav territory. Simultaneously, Serb Nationalists, the Chetniks, perpetrated mass killings in Croatian and Muslim villages. Ethnic nationalism and memories of ethnic violence during the Second World War came to the fore again in the 1990s.[7]

During the Tito regime, the different nationalistic tendencies within Yugoslavia were eclipsed by the call for comradeship and unity among all Yugoslavian peoples under Communism. However, after the death of Tito in 1980, previous tensions and antagonisms began to surface again, with memories of massacres, and fear and suspicion of other ethnic groups rising among the different peoples of Yugoslavia. In 1989, under the rule of the Serbian leader, Slobodan Milošević, Yugoslavia was a federation of six republics (Bosnia-Herzegovina, Croatia, Macedonia, Montenegro, Serbia and Slovenia), as well as two autonomous provinces, Kosovo and Vojvodina (see Map 6). The break-up of this federation in the 1990s produced the most serious conflict in Europe since the end of the Second World War.

**MAP 6** *The Former Yugoslavia.*

# The Break-up of Yugoslavia, Ethnic Cleansing and Genocide

The conflict was multi-sided and multi-ethnic: between Serbia and Croatia; between Serbia and Croatia against Bosnia; and within Bosnia itself, where the situation was made more complex by the presence of large Muslim populations. The process of the break-up of Yugoslavia began with the declaration of independence of Slovenia and Croatia on 25 and 26 June 1991, respectively. This posed a problem for Milošević. If all the republics became independent with their existing borders, the Serbs, who had substantial populations in three of them (Serbia, Croatia and Bosnia), would be divided between three separate countries. Milošević, who had been elected President of Serbia by a large majority in December 1990, was determined to prevent such a situation. On the contrary, his aim was to create a 'Greater Serbia'. Regarding himself as the true defender of Serbian identity and nationhood, Milošević used military might, as well as propaganda, to achieve his aims. Milošević tried to make Croatian independence conditional upon Croatia ceding territories with a Serb majority population, especially the Krajina region. However, the President of Croatia, Franjo Tudjman, refused to acquiesce to this demand. Serbs in Croatia made up 12 per cent of the population. They feared that their position and security would be jeopardised in an independent Croatia. With assistance from Belgrade, Croatian Serb military forces took over one-third of Croatian territory. In Croatia, the first ethnic cleansing campaigns had begun in July 1991. This entailed a war against the population, marked out by 'urbicide' or the destruction of the infrastructure of cities. This was a goal not only to kill and drive out undesirable populations, but also to destroy anything that could be a reminder of their very existence in a region, such as schools and churches. Ethnic cleansing, a term used to denote the elimination of a group of people from a particular location or area, characterised this conflict. The 'multidimensional geopolitics of ethnic cleansing' here were aimed at eradicating a population group and all memory of its existence from a particular area.[8] During this conflict, some 300,000 people became internally displaced and another 200,000 people fled the country.[9] The Croatian Serbs had established the 'Republic of Serbian Krajina' in the territory they had taken. In 1995, Croatian military forces took back this Serb-controlled territory in Operation Oluja. The Croatians, in reprisal, looted and burned many thousands of Serbian homes, killing at least 100 civilians and forcing more than 150,000 Croatian Serbs to leave their homes during a large-scale episode of ethnic cleansing.

The situation in the region deteriorated further when Bosnia had declared independence in April 1992. In response to this, the Bosnian Serbs, led by Radovan Karadžić, with help from Serbia, proclaimed their own separate 'Republika Srpska'.[10] Arkan's Tigers and other Serb paramilitary groups moved into Bosnia, and in May 1992, General Ratko Mladić was named commander of Republika Srpska's army. Mladić brought a high level of professional expertise and ruthlessness to Serb nationalist forces. Simultaneously, Croatia wanted to take over areas of Bosnia that had a Croatian majority population. Bosnia was in a precarious position. Within the Yugoslavian federation, Bosnia could exist and even flourish. But outside it, its fortunes were very different. By 1991, its ethnically mixed population comprised among its largest groups: 44 per cent Bosnian Muslims; 31 per cent Serbs; and 17 per cent Croats. And so, both Serbia and Croatia coveted Bosnia's territory. Both Serbia and Croatia sought to bring their populations into a single state. Indeed, Milošević and Tudjman had held a secret meeting, even before Bosnia claimed its independence, in which they formulated plans for Bosnia's division and, as Adam Jones writes, 'Bosnia became the most brutal battlefield of the Balkan wars'.[11]

The passivity of Western governments' responses to the situation in this region was taken as a green light by Serbia to move on with its ethnic cleansing in Bosnia. In 1992, both Serbians and Croatians engaged in ethnic cleansing campaigns against the Muslims in Bosnia. A massacre fever spread in which all sides involved in the conflicts committed atrocities against each other. There were perpetrators and victims on all sides of these conflicts, but there were great differences in the scale of the atrocities that occurred. Eventually, a series of international interventions took place. The European Union attempted mediation between Serbia and Croatia. A mission led by David Owen from Europe and Cyrus Vance from the USA attempted to negotiate a settlement in Bosnia. In September 1991, the UN had placed an arms embargo on all participants in the conflict. However, this was circumvented in reality. In addition, the UN attempted a humanitarian intervention, sending troops to supply food and medicine to civilian populations in the region. The USA did not take part in this. Those troops that did participate, including French and British, found themselves in a dangerous position.

In 1993, the UN Security Council proclaimed 'safe areas' for civilians and refugees at Sarajevo, Goražde, Srebrenica, Tuzla, Žepa and Bihać, and provided the UNPROFOR (United Nations Protection Force) troops to watch over and guard them, but again, the reality of the situation was that the UN peacekeepers were powerless to provide protection. The capital city, Sarajevo, partly controlled by Bosnian Serb forces, was in a state of siege between March 1992 and December 1995, with Serbian artillery pounding the city from the hills above the city and snipers shooting at civilians. The section of the city not under Serb control was effectively cut off. Its citizens were deprived of food, water and other basic necessities. The UN provided humanitarian aid to try to prevent the people of Sarajevo from starving, but the Serbs often blocked its passage too. Mosques and cultural repositories, including the National Museum and the National Library, were purposefully destroyed.

At Srebrenica alone, 8,372 Bosnian Muslim boys and men were rounded up and massacred between 13 and 15 July 1995.[12] The Dutch UN peacekeeping forces stationed there were unable to protect them. They were inadequately armed and had been instructed only to use force in self-defence. An eyewitness account, from survivor Hakija Huseinović, recalls the massacre of a group of Bosnian Muslim men, who had been rounded up and forced into an agricultural warehouse, where the Serbs shot them en masse:

> As I lay down, the right-hand side of my body got soaked in blood. I couldn't stand it any longer, so I got up from the blood and pulled a dead body underneath me to lie on top of it. When dawn started breaking, [my neighbour] Zulfo Salilović got up to urinate and have a drink of water. I tugged at his coat and told him, "Stay down," and he said, "I can't hold it any longer." A machine-gun burst cut him in half and he fell down. I covered myself with two dead bodies and stayed underneath for twenty-four hours.[13]

He was one of the very few to survive this massacre. Judge Riad of the International Criminal Tribunal for the Former Yugoslavia (ICTY) later described this massacre. These were 'scenes of unimaginable savagery' and 'truly scenes from hell, written on the darkest pages of human history' (see Figure 6). Radislav Krstić, Chief of Staff of the Drina Corps of the Bosnian Serb Army, was sentenced to thirty-five years' imprisonment by the ICTY for his part in the Srebrenica massacre, permitting his soldiers to engage in this grim episode in Bosnia's history.

The process and organisation of Serbia's genocidal campaigns were carefully planned. The hierarchical command structure ensured efficiency in the execution of tasks. The Serbian army entered an area

**FIGURE 6** *Exhumation and identification of Srebrenica victims, Bosnia.*

first, bombing and surrounding villages. Serbian paramilitary forces then moved in to carry out the massacres, with the assistance of local Serbian civilians. As well as being operationally efficient, this separation of tasks was a method used to make individuals feel less culpable as they became engaged in criminal deeds. Furthermore, they worked in closed-off areas. In a restricted theatre of operations, violence became limitless. Jacques Semelin has explained how the 'closed door' became a condition of barbarity.[14] Moreover, the 'closed door' created a culture of impunity. Protected by their hierarchy and unexposed to witnesses, the perpetrators were at liberty to do as they pleased with their victims. The victims were entirely at the mercy of their persecutors. There was no possibility of escape and so the perpetrators had a sense of unlimited power. At Žepa, a safe area taken over by the Serbs in July 1995, General Mladić told his Muslim victims: 'Nothing, nobody, neither Allah nor the UN can help you out. I now am your God.'[15] Violence was partly legitimised on the grounds that it was retribution for crimes carried out formerly by the victim group against the perpetrator group.

At Prijedor, Muslims were forced by Serb nationalists to mark out their homes with white sheets and to wear white armbands. This distinguished them and marked them out as Muslims, making it easier to target them. This action bore marked resemblance to both Nazi and Khmer Rouge policies in relation to the distinguishing of victims in this way, as we saw in Chapters 3 and 5, respectively. The Bosnian Muslims saw the destruction of their mosques all over their country, including the mosque at Banja Luka in 1993, which was a notable example of Ottoman architecture. They suffered mass population expulsions and bloody massacres. Men were separated from women and children in the round-ups in order to heighten fear and minimise the possibility of resistance. The victims were humiliated and dehumanised, described by their persecutors as 'dogs', even as 'cabbages' and 'packets'. The Nazis and the Khmer Rouge similarly used terms that dehumanised their victims, as discussed in earlier chapters, as did the Hutu in Rwanda to describe the Tutsi, as we shall see in the next chapter. At concentration camps, such as the one at Omarska, victims were tortured, beaten and killed. During the course of this war in Bosnia, more than half of its 4.4 million population had been displaced. In addition, Bosnian Serb armed forces and paramilitary groups engaged in mass rape as an instrument of terror. The Serbian forces set up 'rape camps', essentially brothels for Serbian soldiers, in which Bosnian Muslim women were repeatedly raped. Rape was used as a weapon of genocide too, as Muslim women were raped in order to ostracise them from their communities and destroy their ethnic identities. The victims of rape were considered to be tainted and unfit for marriage within their society. In particular, if they fell pregnant they were doubly shunned on returning home, as children born of these rapes were not considered to be members of the community into which they were born. The mass rapes therefore were designed to weaken the ethnic identity of the Bosnian Muslims as a group. The aim of the use of mass rape as an instrument of genocide was to decrease the number of Bosnian children in the next generation.[16] Subsequently, a sense of abject shame prevented the women who had been subjected to rape from speaking about their ordeal.

Finally, in 1995, the USA used the NATO alliance to launch bombing attacks against Serbia and the conflict in Bosnia was brought to an end, but not before a heavy death toll had been amassed and millions of people had been displaced. In November 1995 an agreement was signed at Dayton, Ohio. Milošević, Tudjman and Izetbegović signed the Dayton Accords for Serbia, Croatia and Bosnia respectively. The

Dayton Accords provided for the independence of Bosnia, which was divided into two parts. One part was Serbian and the other part was Croatian and Muslim. Between 1992 and 1995, a death toll of approximately 100,000 people resulted from this ethnic conflict.[17]

Later in the decade, more blood was spilled over Kosovo. This had been an autonomous province of Yugoslavia.[18] Although the vast majority of its population – more than 80 per cent – was Albanian, the Serbs considered the province of Kosovo as their historic homeland. Only in the seventeenth and eighteenth centuries, under renewed pressure from the Ottoman Empire, did Serbs move north in a great migration to Belgrade and the surrounding area. Serbian legend invoked Kosovo as the historic heartland of Serbia. The Ottoman Turks had defeated Serbia in 1389 at Kosovo Polje (The Field of Blackbirds). The 1389 battle against the Turks was regarded as the great national tragedy of the Serbs. Milošević exploited these Serbian nationalist themes with great success. In 1989, he addressed a huge rally to commemorate the 600th anniversary of the battle, evoking heroism and the myth of Greater Serbia to unite the Serbs. Milošević's exclusivist Serb nationalism was ardent and extreme. Many Serbs responded to his calls for Serbian national renewal with great enthusiasm. They came to regard themselves as marginalised, and in order to redress this, Milošević revoked Kosovo's status as an autonomous province, as well as removing Kosovo Albanians from positions of public employment. His harsh measures towards the Albanians resulted in a considerable increase in tensions between Kosovo Albanians and Kosovo Serbs.

In 1996, the Kosovo Liberation Army (KLA) began attacking Serb police forces and established camps where Serbs were detained and tortured. In response, many Kosovo Serbs fled their homes. By 1998, the tensions between Kosovo Albanians and Kosovo Serbs had escalated into an armed struggle. Serbian forces responded to KLA attacks disproportionately, ultimately driving Albanians out of Kosovo. Similarly to earlier Serbian campaigns elsewhere in the region, paramilitary forces worked with Serbian army units to ethnically cleanse the territory, removing ethnic Albanians through systematic acts of terror, violence and mass murder, attacking villages and burning down houses, whilst brutalising their inhabitants. Similarly to the Serbian massacres in Bosnia earlier in the decade, Albanian men were rounded up from villages such as Meja and shot to death. The ethnic cleansing campaign aimed to create a homogeneous Serb majority in Kosovo.

By the end of 1998, international attention among political decision-makers and human rights groups turned to Kosovo. There was heated controversy about whether or not Milošević's actions amounted to genocide. Certainly, the term genocide could be used to smooth the way for the possibility of armed intervention and to galvanise public support for this. However, diplomatic means were attempted first, with the mission by the Organisation for Security and Co-operation in Europe (OSCE) trying to establish an end to the conflict. Despite growing international pressure, however, Serbia refused to sign an agreement to conclude the conflict. At first, the international community hesitated on the question of armed intervention in Kosovo, but eventually decided it was time to take action against Milošević's regime. Between 23 March and 10 June 1999, NATO forces launched a bombing campaign against Serbia on behalf of Kosovo. However, without the mandate of the United Nations Security Council (as Russia had opposed armed intervention), this military intervention raised difficult questions in regard to its legality in terms of international law. It was contentious too because the use of cluster bombs was reported to have hit civilians. Furthermore, the NATO air strikes at first appeared to speed up Serbian efforts to remove Kosovo Albanians from the region. However, Serbia eventually accepted NATO terms and withdrew its forces from Kosovo. The United Nations Security Council established the United Nations Mission in Kosovo (UNMIK) and made it a UN protectorate. It is estimated that approximately 10,000 ethnic Albanians died during this conflict, with another 800,000 Kosovo Albanians being deported to Albania and Macedonia as a result of Serbia's ethnic cleansing campaign in Kosovo. In the aftermath, some half a million refugees were able to return to Kosovo.

# Conclusion

The wars of Yugoslavian secession were not the outcome of ancient hatred. Economic instability in the 1980s was accompanied by the rise of nationalism after Tito's death, and in particular, the deliberate revival and exploitation of painful historical memories from the

Second World War by nationalist leaders. Milošević's nationalism included a sense of displeasure and resentment over previous injustices perpetrated against the Serbs, from Kosovo Polje to the Jasenovac concentration camp in the Second World War, where Croatians had massacred Serbs, as well as Jews and 'Gypsies'. The memory of Jasenovac, in particular, was used by Serbia in the late 1980s and early 1990s for propaganda purposes to frame the struggle between Serbs and Croats.[19] Milošević's nationalism was redemptive, aiming to bring together the dispersed Serbian population into a greater Serbia and to restore the Serb nation to glory, greatness and power. Milošević employed propaganda effectively to inflame tensions between the Serbs and the other ethnic groups in the region, and used military force to bring about his desire to homogenise territory and recast it for Serbian goals.

Nationalists across the republics succeeded in arousing the most deeply held popular grievances and fears. Serb nationalism proved to be the most significant of them. The number of Serbians, the size and power of Serbia and the extent of its claims, as well as the ardency with which nationalists expressed their aims, accounted for this. Serb nationalists put this quite simply: ethnic identities, borders and other populations were obstacles that had to be removed in order for Serbian aims to be achieved. The intention of Serb (and indeed Croat) nationalists was to define categorically who was Serb, who was Croat and who was Muslim, and to determine people's fates based upon this definition. Multinationalism and ethnic co-existence was made unthinkable and unbearable in the efforts of Serb and Croat nationalists to recast the region in the manner they desired. In the end, the issue of international armed intervention, despite heated debates about its legality, made a significant difference. We shall return to questions of genocide prevention, the international community and international law in the final chapter. The following chapter examines the Rwandan genocide that took place in 1994.

# Questions for Further Discussion

1  What motivated the genocidal atrocities in the former Yugoslavia in the 1990s?

2    How did the response of the international community impact these events?

3    Who were the perpetrators?

4    Who were the victims?

5    Why did the conflicts in the former Yugoslavia increase academic and public interest in genocide?

# Further Reading

Baker, C., *The Yugoslav Wars of the 1990s* (London, 2015).

Bećirević, E., *Genocide on the Drina River* (New Haven, CT, 2014).

Bieber, F., Galijas, A. and Archer, R. (eds), *Debating the End of Yugoslavia* (London and New York, 2014).

Biondich, M., *The Balkans: Revolution, War, and Political Violence since 1878* (Oxford, 2011).

Carmichael, C., *Ethnic Cleansing in the Balkans: Nationalism and the Destruction of Tradition* (London, 2002).

Cohen, L. and Dragović-Soso, J. (eds), *State Collapse in South-Eastern Europe: New Perspectives on Yugoslavia's Disintegration* (West Lafayette, IN, 2007).

Dahlman, C. and Toal, G., *Bosnia Remade: Ethnic Cleansing and its Reversal* (Oxford, 2011).

Gagnon, V., *The Myth of Ethnic War: Serbia and Croatia in the 1990s* (Ithaca, NY, 2004).

Glenny, M., *The Fall of Yugoslavia: The Third Balkan War* (London, 1996).

Judah, T., *Kosovo: War and Revenge* (New Haven, CT, 2002).

Judah, T., *Kosovo: What Everyone Needs to Know* (Oxford, 2008).

Mojzes, P., *Balkan Genocides: Holocaust and Ethnic Cleansing in the Twentieth Century* (Lanham, MD, 2011).

Nettelfield, L. and Wagner, S., *Srebrenica in the Aftermath of Genocide* (Cambridge, 2013).

Rohde, D., *Endgame: The Betrayal and Fall of Srebrenica. Europe's Worst Massacre since World War II* (New York, 1997).

Sell, L., *Slobodan Milošević and the Destruction of Yugoslavia* (Durham, NC, 2002).

Sells, M., 'Kosovo Mythology and the Bosnian Genocide', in O. Bartov and P. Mack (eds), *In God's Name: Genocide and Religion in the Twentieth Century* (New York, 2001).

Semelin, J., 'Analysis of a Mass Crime: Ethnic Cleansing in the Former Yugoslavia, 1991–1999', in R. Gellately and B. Kiernan (eds), *The Specter of Genocide: Mass Murder in Historical Perspective* (Cambridge, 2003), pp. 353–70.

Silber, L. and Little, A., *The Death of Yugoslavia* (London, 1998).

# 7

# Genocide in Rwanda

The Rwandan genocide in 1994 was a clear example of a state-sponsored mass murder. Early estimates put the death toll at over 500,000, but more recent works have stated that the figure may have been closer to 1 million. This chapter begins with a discussion of some of the key areas of debate and controversy that surround the Rwandan genocide, continues with an examination of its context and causes, then analyses some of its key features and characteristics. The genocide was an attempt by the Rwandan state and Hutu majority to eliminate each and every last Tutsi. The Tutsi were annihilated during the course of a period of just twelve weeks between April and July 1994. We need to have an understanding of the history of the land in order to find the context for and the causes of the genocide that was unleashed in 1994, for this episode was the result of a number of factors. The genocide was driven by ideological hatred and was aimed at the destruction of the whole of the Tutsi group in the Rwandan population. Where did the seeds of this hatred come from and what were the motivations of the perpetrators?

## Debates and Controversies

There has been controversy surrounding the Rwandan genocide about the nature of the killings, with some commentators depicting them as tribal conflict between atavistic African groups. The original discourse on the Rwandan genocide was shaped by this view, as well as an argument that it was spontaneous, chaotic and disorganised. However, considerable scholarship has debunked concepts of the

Rwandan genocide as the result of old, tribal animosities characterised by frenzied and chaotic violence. René Lemarchand has argued that there is nothing in the historical record to suggest that the genocide resulted from long-standing or deep-seated tribal antagonism.[1] Gérard Prunier also contends that there was 'no trace . . . of systematic violence' between the Tutsi and the Hutu in Rwanda's pre-colonial history.[2] Most scholars now concur that the genocide was not the result of long-standing tribal hatred or atavistic antagonism. The other area of debate surrounds the question of the extent to which the bloodshed was a spontaneous outburst of anger 'from below', or the result of orchestration, organisation and planning 'from above'. The contention that the mass murders were the result of a collective, common outburst of anger unleashed by the shooting down of the President's plane on 6 April 1994 is untenable. Recent scholarly research has shown that the violence was modern, systematic and predetermined. The Hutu leadership planned the genocide, drawing upon, as Scott Straus contends, 'modern, colonially manipulated ethnic categories and a modern ideology of ethnic nationalism'.[3]

# Historical Context

Before the arrival of European colonialists in 1897, Rwanda (see Map 7) had been ruled by a powerful monarchy. The social categories Tutsi and Hutu were notable in this monarchical system. In pre-colonial Rwanda, the term Tutsi referred to herders and the term Hutu referred to agriculturalists. The categories also denoted status and power in Rwandan society. In general terms, Tutsi denoted higher status and Hutu denoted lower status. However, there were variations to these categories – for example, some Hutu reared animals and some Tutsi worked the land; some Tutsi were poor, whilst some Hutu were wealthy. In addition, the social categories were not fixed in the pre-colonial era.

Rwanda came under German colonial rule between 1897 and 1916. This period was followed by an era of Belgian control from 1916 until 1962. Under this European colonial rule, the meaning of these social categories was altered. The Europeans viewed the social

**MAP 7** *Rwanda.*

stratification of Rwandan society in racial terms. They encouraged the domination of society by the Tutsi and introduced a sense of difference between the Hutu and the Tutsi based upon their 'races'. As the colonial powers did not have the necessary resources available to govern Rwandan society, they relied upon local rulers to act on their behalf. First the Germans and then the Belgians came to depend upon the Tutsi king (the *Mwami*) and the Tutsi aristocracy to impose their rule.

The Tutsi and the Hutu were perceived of and labelled as distinct tribes and 'races' by the colonial powers. The Tutsi aristocracy were held to be taller and slimmer than the Hutu peasantry by the European colonisers. The Tutsi had facial features that were closer to the European sense of beauty than those of the Hutu, and so the colonial rulers assumed that the Tutsi were racially superior to the Hutu. Belgian officials and anthropologists claimed that the Tutsi were a conquering 'superior race', originally from Ethiopia, whilst the Hutu were an indigenous, 'inferior race'. The Belgian colonisers employed the 'Hamitic Hypothesis' – propounded first by John Hanning Speke – to legitimise their use of the Tutsi to help them rule. The Hamitic Hypothesis characterised the Hutus as descendants of Ham, the black son of Noah, destined to be inferior, whilst the Tutsi were said to have originated from the Nilotic civilisation of ancient Egypt. The Belgian colonial power regarded the Hutu as unintelligent and inferior, as well as unfit to rule. By contrast, the Belgians viewed the Tutsi as the natural elite of Rwanda. Accordingly, by 1959, they gave forty-three out of forty-five ruling positions to the Tutsi, leaving only two for the Hutu. Indeed, Lemarchand has argued that 'it was the Belgian colonial state that provided the crucible within which ethnic identities were reshaped and mythologized'.[4] For example, the introduction of identity cards showing ethnic backgrounds was introduced in 1933 during the Belgian colonial era.

In addition, the Belgian colonialists introduced a system of compulsory labour. The Hutu had to work for the colonial power without payment. The Belgians took over land from the Hutu without compensation. Belgian colonial practices and policies were distinctly favourable to the Tutsi and simultaneously unfavourable to the Hutu. Many Tutsi converted to Catholicism. They attended the missionary schools run by Belgian priests in order to improve their social standing further, and they did well under Belgian colonial rule. Over time, as the Hutu continued to remain poor and politically powerless, they came to resent not only the Belgian colonial power, but also the Tutsi. Their own sense of worth was low, as their inferiority became entrenched. The Tutsi and Hutu came to accept the European version of their origins and distinctions. The Tutsi basked in the favour they received from the Belgians and came to regard themselves as being superior to the Hutu, just as the Europeans did. As a result, the Hutu came to resent and hate the Tutsi. A racial distinction between the Tutsi and the Hutu emerged. As Straus has noted, colonial rule both racialised a pre-existing social hierarchy and made race 'a central determinant of power'.[5]

In the 1950s, however, the Belgian administration changed its policies, partly due to the arrival of a new generation of Catholic missionaries, bringing with them the ideals of Christian democracy. It attempted to democratise the system of colonial rule and became more sympathetic to the Hutu. By 1957, Hutu political groups began to call for an end to their inferior status and to the Tutsi hegemony. They regarded the Tutsi as 'aliens', not as an indigenous elite. However, they were not concerned with redressing the inequality in the balance of power to make it equal. They intended to tip the scales entirely the other way, so that the Tutsi hegemony would be replaced with Hutu dominance. They believed that the Tutsi should be subordinated and called for the identity cards that showed the racial distinctions between the Tutsi and the Hutu to be continued from the colonial era. Indeed, in 1994, these identity cards facilitated the genocide, as we shall see later in the chapter.

In 1959, the *Mwami* died. Given the changes in their policy, the Belgian authorities aided Hutu political groups in a revolt against Tutsi rule. Tutsi administrative officers were replaced with Hutus. From 1 November 1959, Hutu violence, encouraged by the Belgians, spread across the country. The Hutu revolution changed Rwanda from a Belgian colony that had favoured the Tutsi elite into a Hutu populist democracy. The Belgians were relinquishing their control of Rwanda within a wider process of European decolonisation during this period. The Hutu revolt was a democratic, anti-feudal mass movement, which claimed the Hutu as authentic Rwandans and the Tutsi as a feudal and alien enemy. The Tutsi were excluded from the new political order. Indeed, as Lemarchand has noted, the inversion of the Hamitic Hypothesis, 'emphasizing the foreignness, cunning, and perversity' of the Tutsi as 'feudal exploiters', had played a 'decisive role in legitimizing Hutu ascendancy in the last years of colonial rule'.[6] In October 1960, the Hutu leader Grégoire Kayibanda headed a provisional government. He claimed that 'democracy has vanquished feudalism'. In reality, the Hutu had vanquished the Tutsi, in terms of political power. On 28 January 1961, Rwanda was declared a republic and on 1 July 1962, Kayibanda became President of the newly independent state. The colonial period had ended, but the identity cards that had been introduced under Belgian rule remained. The subsequent Hutu authoritarian political system assigned the Tutsi no place in its undertakings. The new Hutu counter-elite used ethnicity to overturn their previously subordinate political and economic status. There had never been any long-standing tribal rivalry between the Tutsi and the Hutu prior to the colonial era. The violence against the Tutsi following the Hutu revolution caused a mass exodus of Tutsi to the neighbouring countries of Burundi and Uganda. By 1964, there were 336,000 Tutsi refugees. From among this Tutsi diaspora, guerrilla groups were formed to attack Rwanda from abroad. By the start of the 1970s, the Hutu became engaged in pogroms against the Tutsi in Rwanda. In July 1973, President Kayibanda was ousted from power by his army chief of staff, Juvénal Habyarimana. Habyarimana established a one-party dictatorship with his National Revolutionary Movement for Development (MRND). Discrimination against the Tutsi became a matter of course.

In the meantime, the Tutsi diaspora had mobilised. On 1 October 1990, the Rwandan Patriotic Front (RPF), a Tutsi force based in Uganda, began operations that led to an invasion of Rwanda, engaging the Rwandan government in a civil war. This gave the Hutu in the Rwandan government a justification for increasing anti-Tutsi campaigns. The threat posed by the RPF, together with a fear of domestic political opposition, radicalised the Hutu ruling elite, which sought to maintain its power through terror and bloodshed. Ordinary people grew accustomed to the violence. These attacks continued despite the accords reached at the Arusha Conference in Tanzania (July 1992 – August 1993). The Arusha Accords were signed on 4 August 1993 and the UN agreed to oversee their implementation. The Accords guaranteed free elections to be held within two years, to include the RPF, which had been permitted troops in Kigali. The UN sent 2,500 foreign peacekeeping forces (UNAMIR – the United Nations Assistance Mission to Rwanda) to monitor the ceasefire. Another important development was the assassination of Burundi's first Hutu president, Melchior Ndadaye, in October 1993. This was a matter of concern for Hutu extremists in Rwanda, who subsequently established a political alliance known as Hutu Power. This consisted of Hutu hardliners from all political parties.

On 6 April 1994, Habyarimana's plane was shot out of the sky on his return from a trip to Tanzania. Hutu Power, the radical Hutu elite group at the centre of government, used this incident as an opportunity to call for the extermination of the Tutsi. It remains unknown whether the event was orchestrated by Hutu Power or whether it was carried out by the RPF. Either way, the incident was utilised by the Hutu as a pretext for their genocidal campaign against the Tutsi. Hutu Power maintained that they needed to pre-empt and prevent any further attempts by the Tutsi to attack the Hutu. Roadblocks were set up almost immediately around Kigali and subsequently around the country. Hutu Power initiated and orchestrated the genocide against the Tutsi. This power-wielding elite found that the majority of the Hutu population was willing to participate in their mass killing campaign. Economic crisis helped the genocidal cause of the perpetrators, as poor, ordinary Hutu people stood to gain from the opportunity to pillage and plunder the Tutsi targeted for death. This popular participation and involvement for material gain showed marked similarities to other cases we have examined earlier in this book – for example, the Armenian genocide and the Holocaust.

## The Genocide and its Key Features

The genocide began in the country's capital, Kigali. However, it spread across the whole of the country with great swiftness. Hutu Power employed the mass media to mobilise public opinion, both against the Tutsi and against the Hutu opposition. They alleged that both the Tutsi and the moderate Hutu who opposed the killing campaign were traitors. The Tutsi were vilified not only as 'traitors', but also as 'cockroaches'. The label 'cockroach' dehumanised the Tutsi, equating them with pests. We have noted similar tendencies to dehumanise victims in this way in several other cases previously in the book. Such terminology was used to justify the extermination policy. In addition, the Tutsi were demonised and portrayed as 'aliens' who threatened the integrity of the Hutu nation. The mass media, in particular *Radio-Télévision Libre des Mille Collines* (RTLM), spread Hutu propaganda against the Tutsi.[7] *Radio Mille Collines* put out the messages that 'The graves are only all half full' and that 'The enemy is out there – go get him'. The newspaper *Kangura* disseminated similar messages. As 'aliens', the Tutsi could never be part of the Rwandan nation. Furthermore, the Tutsi were portrayed as cunning. As a result, they were a permanent threat to the unsuspecting

Hutu and needed to be exterminated. Such propaganda aimed to frighten the ordinary Hutu into action against the Tutsi.

The mass murder campaign was not directed solely at men, but also at women on the grounds that they would give birth to more Tutsi, and children, who would grow up to become the next generation of the enemy. In this way, the genocide of all Tutsi was justified. Ordinary people were called upon to participate in the killings. Hutu Power prepared the population for genocide in such a way that when the order came to start the killing, the genocide was executed with great alacrity. It was a carefully planned and orchestrated campaign from above, but its success and speed depended upon the level of popular participation that the perpetrators achieved. The enemy was demonised and dehumanised to such an extent that ordinary Hutu participated widely in their mass murder, using hoes, machetes, clubs and other farming implements to massacre their Tutsi neighbours.

The apparatus for the genocide had already been put into place by 1992. It centred on the *akazu* (little house), which consisted of Habyarimana's wife, Agathe, three brothers-in-law and a small group of close advisers who planned the genocide. Killing lists, some of which may have been drawn up as early as 1991, identified prominent Tutsi and those sympathetic to the RPF. Colonel Théoneste Bagosora was a key *génocidaire* (a person involved in perpetrating a genocide). Another important set of protagonists were the organisers across the countryside – between 300 and 500 communal and prefectoral personnel who constituted the middle cadres responsible for supervision of the killings. The ground-level militias that engaged in the mass killings were called the *interahamwe* ('those who stand together'). The *interahamwe* started out as a youth organisation of the ruling MRND party. Swiftly, the *interahamwe*, made up of specially recruited and trained paramilitary forces and comprised of some 50,000 members, became the key perpetrators in the killing, looting and rape of the Tutsi. Furthermore, they played a significant part in encouraging ordinary Hutu civilians (often at gunpoint) to murder their Tutsi neighbours. The presidential guard, comprising about 6,000 men, was recruited and trained to help the *interahamwe* in their mass murder campaign. This cadre was responsible for the immediate killing of members of both the Tutsi and the Hutu opposition in the days following the crash of Habyarimana's plane on

6 April 1994. This massacre in Kigali was the result o.
Colonel Bagosora and other extreme Hutu leaders for an imm
response to the threats to the state posed by the Tutsi. Beginning a
matter of hours after the plane crash, these killings were based on
pre-existing lists. As the genocide spread, and roadblocks were
established, identity cards provided quick evidence of ethnic identity
and facilitated the process of the genocide of the Tutsi. The manner
and speed of the killings suggests careful, advanced planning; the
Rwanda genocide was not at all a spontaneous outburst of anger
directed at the Tutsi after the death of the Hutu president.

Robert Melson has argued that 'the extent of its mass participation'
was a key characteristic of 'the distinctiveness of the Rwandan
genocide'.[8] Men, women and even children actively engaged in the
genocidal killings. Indeed, as Christian Scherrer has noted: 'For the first
time in modern history, a state succeeded in transforming the mass of
its population into murderers.'[9] Why was popular participation so great?
In part, ordinary Hutu men, women and even children were doing what
their government instructed them to do. Furthermore, the propaganda
machine effectively told them to kill or be killed. It instilled into the Hutu
so much fear and dread of the Tutsi enemy that they joined in the killing
frenzy. An ideologically racist view of the Tutsi had become widespread.
The belief that the Tutsi were foreign invaders from Ethiopia who
had arrived many centuries earlier and who wanted to destroy the
Hutu and take their land had become entrenched. As Lemarchand
has noted, the Hamitic Hypothesis provided 'ideological justification
to the *génocidaires*'.[10] The diverse social background of the killers is
noteworthy. Journalists, university lecturers, teachers, doctors and
even priests were accomplices in the massacre of the Tutsi. Landless
Hutu peasants and disaffected city youth joined the killing, fuelled by
the desire to take property or possessions. Greed and bloodlust, as
well as a desire to exercise power over those who had previously
enjoyed a higher social status, motivated these perpetrators. As Prunier
demonstrates:

> They could steal, they could kill with minimum justification, they
> could rape and they could get drunk for free . . . The political aims
> pursued by the masters of this dark carnival were quite beyond
> their scope. They just went along, knowing it would not last.[11]

Hence, as well as soldiers and militias, ordinary men and women engaged in the genocide.[12] Mahmood Mamdani notes that it was this involvement and agency of ordinary Hutus that turned this slaughter into a genocide: 'Without massacres by machete wielding civilian mobs, in the hundreds and thousands, there would have been no genocide.'[13] However, it is significant to note that some Hutu did not participate in the genocidal campaign against the Tutsi. A minority of them tried to save Tutsi victims by hiding them, although by doing so, they were placing themselves in grave danger.

Some of the worst massacres occurred at churches and mission compounds where the Tutsi came to seek refuge, for example, at Nyamata, Musha and Karubamba (see Figure 7). Eyewitness Jean-Baptiste Munyankore tells of the atrocities and those who participated in them:

> What happened in Nyamata, in the churches, in the marshes and on the hills, were the abnormal actions of perfectly normal people. Here's why I say that. The principal and the inspector of schools in my district joined in the killings with nail-studded clubs . . . A priest, the mayor, the assistant chief of police, a doctor – they all killed with their own hands.[14]

**FIGURE 7** *Memorial and massacre site at Nyamata, Rwanda.*

Hospitals, stadia and schools too became sites for large-scale massacres of Tutsi civilians. At Gatwaro stadium in Kibuye prefecture, for example, 12,000 people were killed in a single day.[15] Adam Jones also notes the routinised character of the killings: 'Killers arrived for their duties at a designated hour, and broke off their murderous activities at five in the afternoon, as though clocking off.'[16] Survivor Marie-Louise Kayogire recalls:

They wanted to wipe us out so much that they became obsessed with burning our photo albums during the looting, so that the dead would no longer have a chance to have existed. To be safer, they tried to kill people and their memories . . . They worked for our extermination and to erase all signs of that work, so to speak. Today, many survivors no longer possess one single little photo of their mama, their children, their baptism or marriage, a picture that could have helped them smooth a little sweetness over the pain of their loss.[17]

Extremist Hutu leaders regarded the expulsion or the deportation of the Tutsi as inadequate solutions. They maintained that the attacks in the early 1990s were being carried out by the descendants of Tutsi who had fled or been driven out of Rwanda in the aftermath of the Hutu Revolution of 1959. They were determined not to repeat the 'mistake of 1959' – that is, to allow a new generation of Tutsi to rise. This was an important motivating factor in their decision for genocide. The Tutsi were regarded as 'enemies' and 'traitors'. They did not belong to the nation. They were alleged to be plotting with the RPF against the state. We noted similar arguments about disloyalty to the state made by the Young Turk protagonists against the Armenians in Chapter 2.

Once again, the world looked away as another episode of mass murder unfolded, this time in Africa. Neither the public nor the press showed any real interest in the Rwandan genocide. The clichés about ancient tribal enmity and bloodletting used by the media at the time of the genocide were wholly inappropriate and contributed to international indifference and inaction. They misrepresented the killings as reciprocal atrocities between atavistic, warring African tribes. The immediate evacuation of all Westerners took place. All foreign governments and official bodies, including the UN Security Council, continued to recognise the Hutu government and none of them called upon it to stop the killings. On 5 October 1993, the UN Security Council had set up UNAMIR (United Nations Assistance Mission for Rwanda), in order to assist in the implementation of the Arusha Accords. Its mandate was to monitor the ceasefire agreement, to watch over the security situation before new elections and to help in the coordination of humanitarian aid. A Canadian Force Commander, Roméo Dallaire, who had been unaware of the intentions of the Hutu to massacre outright their Tutsi compatriots, led the mission. On 7 April 1994, ten Belgian peacekeepers who had been protecting the Prime Minister, Agathe Uwilingiyimana, were seized and killed by Hutu militias, along with her. Following these murders, Belgium promptly withdrew its forces from Rwanda, as did other countries. Dallaire, who was left with less than 500 troops, asked for reinforcements. Not only did the UN Security Council refuse this request, but also, on 21 April 1994, it voted to reduce UNAMIR on the grounds that the mission to monitor the peace was now superfluous. The mission was reduced drastically and Dallaire was ordered to leave. Poorly equipped and with limited manpower and resources, Dallaire stayed on and did what he could to help the Tutsi in Rwanda.[18] In June 1994, a French intervention under UN auspices, Opération Turquoise, proved controversial, for whilst it may have saved many lives, its main purpose was to uphold the Hutu Power government, rather than to protect the Tutsi. As the massacres continued, the UN Security Council eventually voted to establish a new mission, UNAMIR II, comprising 5,500 troops. However, it arrived in July 1994, after the RPF under General Paul Kagame had ousted the regime from power and after the genocide had ended on 17 July 1994.

# Conclusion

Whilst the European colonisers invented neither the social stratification in Rwanda nor the ethnonyms Tutsi and Hutu, the impact of European colonial rule did change the meaning of these groups' ethnicity. Ethnic nationalism became the dominant political ideology of the Hutu after independence. Assertions that ancient tribal hatred caused the genocide are unhelpful in trying to ascertain its origins. The genocide in Rwanda in 1994 was not spontaneous, chaotic and disorderly. In contrast, it was duly planned and organised from above, using the apparatus of the state and the media, to carry out and promote the mass murder of the Tutsi. As Straus has asserted, 'the violence was top-down, systematic, intentional, and state driven.'[19]

The unwillingness of the international political community to intervene in Rwanda meant that the Hutu perpetrators had not only the motives and means, but also the opportunity to execute their plans. They drank champagne and toasted to a future without the Tutsi. The extent of mass popular participation and the speed with which the mass murder of the Tutsi minority took place are the most noteworthy and distinctive features of the Rwandan genocide. The genocide in Rwanda was a paradigmatic case, crucial to the field of genocide studies. Debates on its origins, the way in which it was carried out and the response of the international community to it have generated considerable attention to the Rwandan genocide, which was comparatively short lived, yet so fast and far reaching in its brutality and consequences. In the next chapter, we turn to another genocide on the African continent, in the Darfur region of Sudan, during the first decade of the twenty-first century.

## Questions for Further Discussion

1 Why have the origins of the Rwandan genocide generated so much academic debate?

2 What were the most distinctive characteristics of the Rwandan genocide?

3 Who were the perpetrators and what were their motives?

4 Why was the international response to the genocide so ineffective?

# Further Reading

Barnett, M., *Eyewitness to a Genocide: The United Nations and Rwanda* (Ithaca, NY, 2002).

Dallaire, R., *Shake Hands with the Devil: The Failure of Humanity in Rwanda* (New York, 2004).

Destexhe, A., *Rwanda and Genocide in the Twentieth Century* (New York, 1995).

Hatzfeld, J., *Life Laid Bare: The Survivors in Rwanda Speak* (New York, 2007).

Mamdani, M., *When Victims Become Killers: Colonialism, Nativism, and the Genocide in Rwanda* (Princeton, NJ, 2001).

Melvern, L., *A People Betrayed: The Role of the West in Rwanda's Genocide* (London, 2000).

Melvern, L., *Conspiracy to Murder: The Rwandan Genocide* (London, 2004).

Prunier, G., *The Rwanda Crisis: History of a Genocide* (New York, 1995).

Straus, S., *The Order of Genocide: Race, Power, and War in Rwanda* (Ithaca, NY, 2006).

Straus, S., 'The Historiography of the Rwandan Genocide', in D. Stone (ed.), *The Historiography of Genocide* (Basingstoke, 2010), pp. 517–42.

# 8

# Genocide in Sudan

In Sudan, the first genocide of the twenty-first century unfolded in a conflict in the region of Darfur that began in 2003. This arose from long-standing tensions over land, between Arab pastoralists and settled African agriculturalists. The strained relationship between them had intensified as a result of drought and increasing aridity of the land. Arab pastoralists moved southwards from the dry, northern part of Darfur, into territories occupied by the Fur, Massalit and Zaghawa tribes. This movement was seasonal, but exacerbated by desertification. A series of violent clashes was exacerbated by the Khartoum government, which sided with the Arab pastoralists, supplying them with arms. In response, the Sudan Liberation Army (SLA), a rebel group, launched its own insurgency for the failure of the government to offer protection to these groups against Arab raiders. Sudanese government troops and Arab militias attacked village after village in retaliation for rebel attacks on government installations. However, their actions went far beyond avenging the rebel groups alone, to mass atrocities against innocent men, women and children across the region. Martin Daly has described this as 'a devastating response', with seemingly limitless destruction.[1] Families were uprooted and starved to death, children tormented and murdered, and women raped with impunity.

Mahmood Mamdani notes that the victims were 'identified as members of groups', rather than being targeted as individuals.[2] Yet the debate on whether or not the crisis in Darfur amounted to genocide has been fierce. This debate also had implications on the legal requirements for an international response.[3] How and why these crimes continued to rumble on (and were allowed to do so) over the course of several years are the main questions of debate in relation to Darfur. In addition, Carol Gallo notes that it is crucial to understand differences in economic and social structures in Sudan, which are so different from those in which international policies and scholarship in the West are formulated.[4] Once again, as in the cases of the former Yugoslavia and Rwanda that we explored in the previous two chapters, the question of whether or not ancient ethnic hatred provided the catalyst for violence is the subject of both academic debate and popular discourse surrounding the subject of the genocide in Darfur. Khartoum's savage campaign of ethnic cleansing was intended to drive out the peoples of Darfur and to replace them with Arab settlers. The Sudanese government was responsible for the perpetration of atrocities against the local populations in this region. Arab militias, known as the *Janjaweed* (men on horseback) terrorised the peoples here. Their actions were characterised by burning, rape, pillage and the mass murder of entire communities. This chapter considers the context and causes, key features and consequences of the genocide in Darfur.

## Context and Causes

It is essential to understand the history of the area in order to comprehend the origins of the Darfur genocide. It is important to take into account the complex and diverse social structures of the region. For example, constructions of race in Sudan were complex and fluid, with a long-standing and nuanced Arab-African dichotomy, in which identification and self-identification in terms of language, culture and ethnic identity could change.[5] Economic status and lifestyle were also not always fixed, but fluid. Thus, Darfur was a diverse region comprised of changeable ethnic identities. Darfur was established as a sultanate in 1650. It was dominated by the Fur and comprised of a ruling elite that included members of all the principal ethnic groups in Darfur.[6] Most disputes were managed at family or community level through traditional practices during this period. A balance of power was maintained over more than two centuries, until 1874, when al-Zubayr Rahman Mansur, an Arab slave trader, created a personal fiefdom in southern Sudan, destroying the Fur Sultanate. This opened up pastures and areas for cultivation to the Baqqara Arab nomads. Sultan Ali Dinar restored the Fur Sultanate in 1898 and drove the Arab nomads away from the heartland of his realm. Ali Dinar was killed by a British Expeditionary Force in 1916 and Darfur was annexed to the Anglo-Egyptian Condominium (1898–1956), but the British soon realised that the region was poor in resources. Improvements in health provision and education that were introduced by the British into other parts of Sudan did not reach Darfur. The *awlad al-bahar* – descendants of Arab migrants into the Nile Valley, who had entered Sudan during the sixteenth and seventeenth centuries – became a ruling elite class during the five decades of British rule. In 1956, upon the achievement of Sudanese independence from British colonial control, some of the old Darfur elites rejoined political life. However, ethnic and cultural discrimination became an established pattern of governance by the *awlad al-bahar*. For more than two centuries, there had been no central government rule over Darfur. As Robert Collins notes, 'the fundamental reason for fragile governance in Darfur' was the adoption of 'a policy of benign neglect' on the part of the central government in Sudan.[7] Ethnic tensions were a historically extant and accepted part of the way of life in Darfur, exacerbated by competition for pastureland, agricultural land and water sources. Eruptions of violence were not unknown.

Drought in the 1980s heightened competition to an unprecedented level, when camel nomads from areas to the north moved southwards into this region. Decreases in soil quality and land productivity added to the difficulties experienced in Darfur. As Gallo notes: 'Over-farming and over-grazing led to depletion of soil quality and land exhaustion.'[8] Whilst disputes had previously been solved by conferences and arbitration, the introduction of automatic weapons into the region eroded these traditional and peaceable methods. This significantly altered social structures and conflict resolution mechanisms in Darfur. As Collins states: 'By the 1990s, Darfur was short of water but awash in guns.'[9] Customary procedures for stopping violence and mediating conflicts were no longer workable. As conflict between groups became greater, people in this region 'whose identity was primarily locally situated suddenly had to identify themselves as Arab or African' in a new set of racio-political categories.[10] Growing competition for the natural resources in Darfur (water and land), the

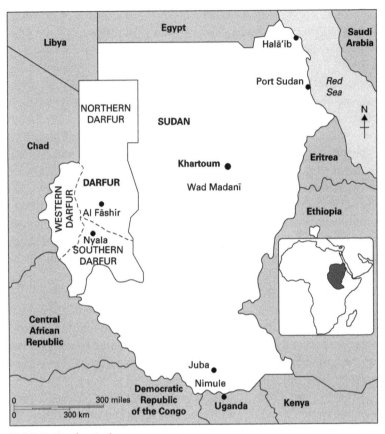

**MAP 8** *Darfur, Sudan.*

impact of desertification and drought, provided the backdrop to this conflict (see Map 8).

On 30 June 1989, Omar al-Bashir gained power in Sudan, utilising the military forces of the National Islamic Front (NIF) and the Popular Defence Forces (PDF) to forcibly institute the Islamisation of the country. Al-Bashir's regime aimed to impose strict Islamist ideology, Arabic culture, dress and language across the whole state. By 1991, 150,000 recruits were conscripted into the PDF. They engaged in attempts to crush the Sudan People's Liberation Army (SPLA) forces in southern Sudan. The SPLA had been established in 1983, as a result of long-standing discontent and antagonism in the south of

Sudan, with its mainly Christian and animist population, about control of the country's resources, as well as the introduction of Islamic *sharia* law by the Islamic north, and which had initiated a civil war in Sudan. In response to their successful incursions, the Sudanese Prime Minister, Sadiq al-Mahdi, had armed the PDF with automatic weapons and gave his Baqqara supporters carte blanche to pillage, rape and kill the ethnic Dinka people who supported the SPLA. The unruly Baqqara militias continued to receive assistance and armaments from Khartoum. Rape, enslavement and killing came to characterise the actions carried out by a variety of Arab militias on behalf of the Sudanese government to those sections of Sudanese society that were black or non-Arabic. In August 2002, when the Sudanese government held a Fur Leadership conference with 129 Fur delegates, Daly notes that even as the conference was underway, the government was making plans to expand assistance to the *Janjaweed*.[11] Essentially, as Alex de Waal notes, 'the Sudan government made a deal with these Arab groups whereby they were allowed to pursue their own agenda with impunity, in return for suppressing the rebellion.'[12]

In February 2003, 300 rebels, led by Abd al-Wahid Ahmad Nur and calling themselves the Darfur Liberation Front (DLF), raided the town of Gulu in western Darfur. Attacking police and government soldiers with automatic weapons and mortars, they seized control of Gulu. Subsequently, under the new name Sudan Liberation Movement (SLM), with its forces named the Sudan Liberation Army (SLA), the rebels demanded 'a united democratic Sudan' with 'full acknowledgement of Sudan's ethnic, cultural, social and political diversity'.[13] Government armed forces were not ready to fight a major rising in western Sudan and so opened negotiations with the SLA. A fragile ceasefire was destroyed, however, following the assassination of Shaykh Saleh Dakoro, a revered Massalit leader, on 18 March 2003. The government forces destroyed the town of Karnoi. On 25 March 2003, the SLA responded by taking the strategic town of Tine, on the border with Chad. The fighting continued throughout Western Darfur, between the SLA, supported by the Justice and Equality Movement (JEM), and the Sudanese army. Attacks by rebels on government buildings and military bases provoked retaliation from Khartoum. SLA successes highlighted the weakness of the Sudanese army.[14] The government of Sudan continued to arm Arab militias in order to bolster its flagging army. The regime also exploited ethnic tensions in the region by branding the rising as an African effort to eliminate the 'Arab race' from Darfur.

# The Genocide and its Consequences

The *Janjaweed* were initially comprised of the sons of the former Baqqara. Convicts, fugitives and desperadoes joined their ranks.[15] The ethnic cleansing campaigns of the *Janjaweed* had started as early as October 2002. They trained in special camps in southern Darfur and were equipped and armed by the Sudanese army. The Fur people became the first group targeted by the *Janjaweed*. The Sudanese armed forces worked in tandem with the *Janjaweed*, providing air support for their surprise raids on Darfur villages and towns, by means of bombing, strafing and furnishing transportation and armaments.[16] The pattern of their actions was uniform and was repeated time and again throughout the region. First, they entered a village just before daybreak, mutilating and killing the men. Then they raped the women and sometimes abducted the children. Daly notes: 'In some cases, women and girls, after rape, were branded to make permanently visible their humiliation; in others they were abducted, ravished over time, then released or killed depending on the whim of their tormentors.'[17] Sometimes 'men and boys were lined up and executed', whilst others were 'led off, never to be seen again'.[18] The *Janjaweed* seized any livestock and then proceeded to burn down the village, as Collins states, 'in a systematic scheme to drive the African population from their ancestral holdings'.[19] The *Janjaweed* verbally abused their victims too, calling them *zurqa* (black) and *abid* (slave), and asserting Arab ownership of the land.[20] The *Janjaweed* destroyed everything in their path and ethnically cleansed the land to make it free for Arab settlement. Their genocidal actions against the Fur people were subsequently repeated against the Massalit and Zaghawa populations in Darfur. These groups too were targeted because of their ethnic heritage. The *Janjaweed* continued their raids and incursions throughout the summer and autumn of 2003 (see Figure 8). A further ceasefire was proposed in September 2003, but

**FIGURE 8** *Remnants of a village destroyed by the* Janjaweed *in Darfur, Sudan.*

it disintegrated very rapidly and the fighting continued. The SLA had some successes against the *Janjaweed*, but these were followed by redoubled efforts on the part of the latter to hunt down and pursue civilians from the targeted ethnic groups.

One survivor, from the village of Tolos in West Darfur, recalls the day when the *Janjaweed* attacked her village:

> In the morning, early, we were taking breakfast, and we heard the planes . . . The planes came first, then the trucks, and then the horses and camels. Some were on foot. The planes, Antonovs, flew over the village . . . Everything caught fire, buildings, animals, people . . . Most *Janjaweed* rode horses, camels or were on foot . . . I was so fearful, I didn't stop running and I was hysterical, crying and running. After the attack, we came back to our village and we found the dead bodies.

She continues her recollection that after her return to her village she found nothing but corpses:

Our animals, our cows, our sorghum, our millet, our clothes, nothing was left. Nothing. It was all burnt, destroyed. The whole village was destroyed.

She further describes the rape of female victims, when she was out collecting wood with five women and three teenage girls:

When we first arrived at the area with the wood, the *Janjaweed*, about twenty of them, were on camels and horses and came up on us very quickly. Some of them said, 'We already took your land, why are you around here? We use your land and now we are going to use you.' We all started running away and four of us got captured, three girls and one woman . . . From the morning until the evening the *Janjaweed* kept the girls and the woman . . . The girls were raped by many men, some by five, some by ten.[21]

Another victim of Massalit ethnicity tells of the (similar) circumstances of the arrival of the *Janjaweed* in her village:

The government used planes and trucks to attack us and the *Janjaweed* came on horses and camels and on foot. They came in the early morning just before sunrise and I was asleep. I first knew there was an attack because I heard the sound of weapons from the planes and the trucks. As soon as I heard sounds I got up and ran from the hut . . . The soldiers and *Janjaweed* chased us and they kept shooting men and boys. Many were killed. They also caught men and slashed them with long knives on the legs and arms, cutting off their arms and legs.[22]

It took until September 2003 for the enormity of the devastation and displacement to be noticed by international aid agencies. In October 2003, *Médecins sans Frontières* (MSF) reported that thousands of Internally Displaced Persons (IDPs) had been traumatised by the brutalities carried out in Darfur by the *Janjaweed*. By means of 'manipulative obstruction', the Sudanese government blocked UN and humanitarian agencies from entering Darfur. In December 2003, Tom Vraalsen, the UN Secretary General's Special Envoy for Humanitarian Affairs, stated that due to this deliberate obstructionism on the part of the Khartoum government, humanitarian operations and relief assistance were virtually impossible. The Centre for Humanitarian Dialogue in Geneva attempted to broker an agreement for humanitarian aid. Whilst the SLM and JEM agreed, Khartoum refused, claiming that 'the issue of humanitarian access had been politicised, used for military gains, and was subject to manipulations'.[23] The Sudanese government continued to obstruct relief efforts. Western governments vacillated in their response, even after UN officials declared the situation in Darfur as the worst humanitarian crisis in the world.

On 7 April 2004, the day commemorating the tenth anniversary of the Rwandan genocide, UN Secretary General Kofi Annan declared that if full humanitarian access continued to be denied in Darfur, then 'the international community must be prepared to take swift and appropriate action . . . which may include military action . . . The international community cannot stand idle.'[24] In the meantime, a ceasefire, mediated by Chad, was signed with the intention of facilitating humanitarian aid to affected populations. Furthermore, the government of Sudan was to put an end to the activities of the armed militias.[25] All in all, however, the Sudanese government expertly exploited the situation caused by ensuing divisions and tensions among both international observers and the rebel groups. In practical terms too, the government put into place bureaucratic measures to stop humanitarian assistance from reaching Darfur. Multiple delaying tactics included 'travel periods, fuel permits, safety tests for drugs, customs delays of vehicles, minute enforcement of detailed regulation'.[26] In addition, food aid was often confiscated, stolen or fed to animals. Despite ongoing international demands for the *Janjaweed* to be disarmed, Sudan's Foreign Minister, Mustafa Ismail, refused to do so. The Sudanese government had no desire to disarm the *Janjaweed* militias or to bring them under control. On the contrary, the president showed his support for the *Janjaweed* by watching them on parade in Nyala on 19 May 2004. The condemnation by the UN Security Council on attacks and atrocities committed by the *Janjaweed* and calls for the government to disarm them fell on deaf ears. The Sudanese government eased some restrictions on humanitarian access to Darfur, but it was still a difficult process.[27]

Despite the featuring of the plight of civilians in Darfur by the international media throughout the summer of 2004 and calls for governments in Europe and the USA to take action, the policy response from the West remained negligible and ineffectual. The USA was unwilling to commit troops to Sudan as it was already committed in Iraq and Afghanistan. America's rejection of the idea of military intervention greatly reduced the impact of any international response.[28] The UN called upon the African Union (AU) to redeem the situation, but the Sudanese government would not accept the presence of any AU peacekeepers. In July, the United Nations Security Council passed Resolution 1556, which demanded the Sudanese government to disarm the *Janjaweed* and arrest its leaders, to cease all military operations and to report back to the Security Council within thirty days. Whilst humanitarian relief efforts began to reach many more IDPs during this period, on 20 August 2004, Kofi Annan concluded that the Sudanese government had not fulfilled the requirements of Resolution 1556. On 30 August 2004, he called for the expansion of the African Union Mission to Sudan (AUMIS).

In August 2004, the pattern of genocidal atrocities committed by the *Janjaweed* militias and government forces against non-Arab villagers continued. Like the United Nations, the USA asked for the rapid deployment of AU troops in Sudan.[29] Neither the UN nor the USA was willing to intervene militarily. The lack of resources permitted to enter Darfur exacerbated a dire situation of genocide by attrition. Mukesh Kapila described the conflict as 'the world's worst humanitarian crisis',[30] and Roméo Dallaire called the events in Sudan 'Rwanda in slow motion'. Prunier notes that as there were no major 'political, economic or security stakes' for the Western world, 'the deaths of human beings' were allowed to continue as attention turned quickly away from events in Darfur.[31] Al-Bashir denied that genocide was taking place and claimed that foreigners had deliberately exaggerated the conflict and inflated casualty and death tolls.

The *Janjaweed* had burned to the ground hundreds of villages, killed thousands of people, engaged in the mass rape of women and abducted children from the targeted communities. The *Janjaweed* forces, made up of Arab-speaking mercenary fighters, often criminals who had been released from prison, attacked the non-Arab villages of the region with great brutality, clearing the land for Arab settlement.[32] The victims were targeted on account of their ethnicity. The systematic destruction signified the intentional elimination of specific ethnic and racial groups, some of whom fled to refuge in neighbouring countries. Thus 'ethnic cleansing' of the area was accomplished. The mass and gang rape of women was also aimed at destroying the targeted groups, with the intention that the victims would give birth to 'light-skinned' children. Mass murder, mass rape, mass starvation and the driving of the Fur, Massalit and Zaghawa peoples off their ancestral lands constituted genocide. Although exact numbers are hotly contested, it is estimated that the conflict, ethnic cleansing and displacement of targeted groups in the region of Darfur claimed at least 200,000 lives (with some sources stating a figure of 300,000) and forced more than 1 million people (maybe as many as 2 million) from their lands as IDPs, with another 200,000 people seeking refuge across the border in Chad.

The Darfur Atrocities Documentation Team (ADT) interviewed more than 1,200 refugees from Darfur over a five-week period in July and August 2004. Of those interviewed by the ADT, 61 per cent stated that they had witnessed the killing of at least one member of their family. A further 16 per cent stated that they had been raped or had been told of a rape directly by the victim. However, shame, humiliation and fear meant that many women and girls did not speak of their ordeals. Relying substantially on this information, US Secretary of State, Colin Powell, stood before the US Senate Foreign Relations Committee on 9 September 2004 and announced that 'genocide has occurred in Darfur and may still be occurring'. This official accusation by the USA that the government of Sudan was perpetrating genocide was 'historic'.[33] It was the first time that a government invoked Chapter VIII of the United Nations Convention on Prevention and Punishment of the Crime of Genocide, calling upon the Security Council to take action.

On 18 September 2004, the United Nations Security Council passed Resolution 1564, calling for 'the immediate establishment of an international commission of enquiry into the situation in Darfur'. This was the first time that the UN had undertaken an investigation to determine whether genocide was being committed by a member state. Furthermore, the UN Security Council referred the case to the International Criminal Court (ICC). In 2008, Luis Moreno Ocampo, the Prosecutor of the ICC, accused President al-Bashir of committing genocide, war crimes and crimes against humanity, and claimed that he was individually criminally responsible for these actions. In July 2010, al-Bashir was indicted by the ICC, which issued a warrant for his arrest. However, he evaded this contemptuously and kept his position as President of Sudan; furthermore, no state he visited after the indictment arrested him.

In the meantime, UN Resolution 1769 of 31 July 2007, after considerable delay and wrangling, mandated a hybrid AU-UN force, the UN-African Union Mission in Darfur (UNAMID). Hence, between 2004 and 2007, the international community pursued a range of objectives for Darfur, but it was exactly this multiplicity of goals – often unrealistic – that impeded a clear strategy. As Alex de Waal explains: 'With an internally dysfunctional regime facing a confused and inconsistent international community, it is unsurprising that little progress was made.'[34] In regard to military intervention, there were debates about whether forces should be under AU or UN command, about the number of troops and their capabilities, about what their mandate should be and about how to finance them. Whilst all of these issues were debated, very little attention was given to the overall strategic aim. Certainly, all efforts fell short of a 'responsibility to protect'. The international community failed to develop sufficient provisions for ceasefire, disarmament and civilian protection in Darfur. Between the USA, the UN and the AU, in the case of Darfur, Mamdani contends that 'the real disagreement was not over the scale of the violence and the destruction it had wrought but over what to call it'.[35] Furthermore, as Daly argues, the international response had been 'unconscionably late'.[36] This was particularly the case because as the civil war in the south of Sudan became the focus of the international community and diplomatic relations, the situation in Darfur received 'scant attention'.[37] In 2005, a peace agreement was reached in which South Sudan was given the right to self-determination in a referendum to be held six years later. Yet the war in the south had had an impact on the situation in Darfur.

# Conclusion

As Prunier maintains, 'For the world at large Darfur was and remained the quintessential "African crisis": distant, esoteric, extremely violent, rooted in complex ethnic and historical factors which few understood, and devoid of any identifiable practical interest for the rich countries.'[38] Indeed, the failure of attempts to intervene effectively in Darfur was the result of a combination of factors, including the lack of a strong mandate, the lack of a realistic concept of operations, insufficient numbers and inadequate financing. Responses of the UN Security Council and the AU consisted, as Alex de Waal notes, of 'ad hoc steps rather than a systematic or strategic approach to the crisis'.[39] Ultimately, the peoples of Darfur had endured devastation and intentional destruction, on grounds of their ethnicity, that amounted to genocide. The Fur, Massalit and Zaghawa groups had distinct languages and cultures, and were distinguished from the Arab perpetrators by their ethnicity. The semantic question on whether or not to use the word 'genocide' to describe what occurred in Darfur had a significant consequence in terms of the international response, but the use of the label genocide per se should not be important. Whether we label it or explain it as tribal conflict, counterinsurgency, ethnic cleansing or genocide, the outcome for the victims amounted to the same thing – an enormous loss of life. In addition to the death toll estimated at 200,000 people, many thousands of villages were entirely destroyed and at least 1 million people were displaced. The next and final chapter explores a number of critical, overarching debates in relation to the subject of genocide.

## Questions for Further Discussion

1  Why did this genocide in Sudan occur?

2  Who were the perpetrators and who were the victims?

3  Why did the genocidal violence continue for so long?

4  To what extent did the international community respond differently to the Darfur genocide than it did to previous cases of genocide?

# Further Reading

Ahmed, A. and Manger, L. (eds), *Understanding the Crisis in Darfur: Listening to Sudanese Voices* (Bergen, 2006).

Daly, M., *Darfur's Sorrow: The Forgotten History of a Humanitarian Disaster* (Cambridge, 2010).

Flint, J. and de Waal, A., *Darfur: A New History of a Long War* (London, 2008).

Grzyb, A. (ed.), *The World and Darfur: International Response to Crimes against Humanity in Western Sudan* (Montreal, 2010).

Hagen, J. and Rymond-Richmond, W., *Darfur and the Crime of Genocide* (Cambridge, 2009).

Hassan, S. and Ray, C. (eds), *Darfur and the Crisis of Governance in Sudan: A Critical Reader* (Ithaca, NY, 2009).

Jeffries, W. (ed.), *The Darfur Crisis* (New York, 2008).

Prunier, G., *Darfur: A 21st Century Genocide* (Ithaca, NY, 2008).

Rottenburg, R. (ed.), *Nomadic-Sedentary Relations and Failing State Institutions in Darfur and Kordofan (Sudan)* (Halle, 2008).

Steidle, B. and Steidle Wallace, G., *The Devil Came on Horseback: Bearing Witness to the Genocide in Darfur* (New York, 2007).

Straus, S., 'Darfur and the Genocide Debate', *Foreign Affairs* Vol. 84, No. 1 (2005), pp. 123–33.

Straus, S., *Making and Unmaking Nations: War, Leadership, and Genocide in Modern Africa* (Ithaca, NY, 2015).

Totten, S. and Markussen, E. (eds), *Genocide in Darfur: Investigating the Atrocities in the Sudan* (New York and London, 2006).

Waal, A. de, (ed.), *War in Darfur and the Search for Peace* (Cambridge, MA, 2007).

# 9

# Themes

Having examined the histories and debates surrounding a selection of canonical genocides, this final chapter analyses four themes pertaining to the subject of genocide that merit further attention here due to the controversies and debates that they have precipitated. Firstly, this chapter treats the subject of gender and genocide. The use of gender as a lens through which to view genocide is a comparatively recent development in the scholarly literature, which has engendered some debate and which has advanced our understanding of the subject. Secondly, this chapter examines debates about genocide prevention and intervention. The question of intervention is always fraught with controversy in academic, political, media and public arenas, and the issue of prevention remains a challenge for our future world. Thirdly, this chapter discusses justice and genocide. To be sure, justice is a crucial issue, yet it is also one that divides opinion. Finally, this chapter considers memory and memorialisation. How genocides reside in popular and collective memory and how traumatised societies and communities memorialise and commemorate genocidal events are also significant subjects and ones that court controversy.

## Gender and Genocide

As we have seen, there have been distinctive approaches to the subject of genocide and different angles of research. Comparatively recently, a gendered perspective has been applied to the subject, in relation to both perpetrators and victims. At first, there was some debate and even hostility towards the use of studying gendered aspects of genocide. Some writers contended that it trivialised the subject. However, research on gender and genocide has expanded considerably, and the fruits of this research have demonstrated that this is not the case at all. Gender-based distinctions provide a useful analytical tool in the discussion of genocides. They allow us to conceptualise gender as a relational identity that affects both women's and men's perceptions of themselves and of each other. Amy Randall contends that perpetrators produced 'gender specific traumas' or 'gendered harms'.[1] Gender plays an important role in shaping both individual and group attitudes and behaviours during episodes of genocide.

As Adam Jones has noted, the perspective of gender allows us to define how men and women are targeted during episodes of genocidal violence.[2] It also enables us to develop a more nuanced understanding of the experiences of both men and women as victims, as well as perpetrators. Recent writing in the field of genocide studies has demonstrated that whilst examinations of sexual violence and genocidal rape have tended to focus much on female victims, gender-specific genocidal acts of violence and sexual violation have also targeted male victims.[3] Furthermore, the field has been advanced by the work of Elisa von Joeden-Forgey on 'genocidal masculinity' and the work of Paula Drumond on the context and nature of sexual violence in war and genocide. In addition, recent work by Nicole Hogg and Mark Drumbl has shown the extent of women as perpetrators in the Rwandan genocide and examined their motives. An analysis of women as perpetrators has been missing from the fields of both Holocaust and genocide studies until comparatively recently.

Joeden-Forgey argues that *génocidaires* often view themselves 'in highly gendered ways' and that 'the crime of genocide is tied to the exertion of a specifically genocidal concept of masculine power on the world'.[4] She conceptualises this as 'genocidal masculinity', a 'form of male domination that both rejects the old patriarchy and embraces an expression of power based on killing rather than life-giving'.[5] In terms of perpetration, Joeden-Forgey argues the importance of conceptualising genocide as a crime committed mainly by men. As Joane Nagel has stated, many key historical processes such as state power, militarism, nationalism, revolution, political violence and dictatorship are 'best understood as masculinist projects, involving masculine institutions, masculine processes and masculine activities', rather than being gender neutral.[6] Joeden-Forgey argues that genocide is also a mainly masculine project. She states that masculinity defines what men should be and how they are meant to act in a gender-specific manner, including types of behaviour such as virility and toughness, which are traditionally associated with men, as well as establishing social, economic and political agendas.[7] Hence, *génocidaires* 'seek permanently to organise society around the task of killing', thereby creating 'a very specific culture that is characterised by the valorisation of pure martial brutality and cold heartedness in men, especially toward "outsiders"'.[8] Joeden-Forgey concludes that the aim of the perpetrators of genocide – based on the concept of 'genocidal masculinity', in turn – is not only 'to destroy the human bodies and other material evidence of a group, but also to get at the very life force responsible for that group's existence'.[9]

Drumond notes that gender-based violence is often used to weaken the social fabric of targeted groups. She argues that '*génocidaires* perpetrate crimes informed by gendered constructions, thereby affirming their group identity as superior in power and masculine prowess'.[10] The crimes of genocide demonstrate particular constructions of gender, both masculinity and femininity. In this regard, Drumond acknowledges that 'the concept of gendercide is relevant not only because it addresses how social constructions of gender influence the dynamics of conflict, but also because it offers a neutral term that addresses both male and female victimisation'.[11] In addition, discourses of masculinity have contributed to the transformation of ordinary boys and men into perpetrators of genocide.

Sexual violence becomes a military weapon that is purposefully employed as a means of control and a political weapon that seeks to destroy the foundation of the victim's sense of self and the world, and his or her community, and simultaneously, to enhance the perpetrator's sense of self and the world. A common feature of constructed gender norms is that they identify masculinity with strength and equate this with bodily power and the capacity for violence. Using these criteria of strength, women are gendered as weak. Men and women are then related to each other through the category of protection. A man establishes his masculinity, at least in part, through his capacity to protect his women and through his ability to defend them against the violence of other men. This makes women vulnerable to the violence of men – as potential victims who become real victims if there are no men to protect them. This symbolic structure can have significant consequences in circumstances of war and conflict. We have noted this in several cases throughout the book, especially clearly exemplified in Bosnia (Chapter 6). Women's bodies can be transformed into weapons of war, not only because their bodies are weaker than those of men, but also because raping them takes away the masculinity from their men as protectors of their communities. In addition, the reproductive powers of women's bodies are controlled by the perpetrators, as illustrated in the case of Bosnian Serbs, who raped Bosnian Muslim women and claimed that the children born of these rapes would be Bosnian Serbs.[12] This point is true also for children born of rape in other genocidal cases too, such as the Armenian genocide and the Rwandan genocide, as we saw in Chapters 2 and 7 respectively.

In traditional wars, the objective was to defeat the enemy. In genocidal wars, the objective was to destroy the enemy. In traditional wars, the enemy was the army of another state or governing body. There was a soldier–civilian distinction. Genocidal wars did not make this distinction; here the enemy was the people – all the people, each and every member of the victim group. There were no protected innocents, as in traditional warfare. In genocidal wars, terrorising the enemy population was insufficient. Humiliation emerged as a key tactic and sexual violence became a high priority. Sexual violence was regarded as an extremely effective way of humiliating, demoralising and dehumanising an ethnic group – of demonstrating that they were unworthy of existence. Beyond the use of torture and murder to terrorise a population, use of rape humiliated an ethnic group. A raped woman was regarded as degraded completely – she was a humiliation to herself, her men and her community. Moreover, 'enemy' women were particularly targeted for sexual violence by militaries because of their importance in constructing and maintaining the ethno-national group. Because of women's role as biological reproducers of the collectivity, as reproducers and as transmitters of culture, they often have been targeted in efforts to destroy a group or to assert dominance over it.

In some genocidal cases, sexual violence against the enemy appears to have been so widespread and systematic that it is hard not to view it as a deliberate military strategy. Mass rape and other forms of sexual violence were used strategically in a variety of instances, including the former Yugoslavia, Rwanda and Sudan, as we have seen in the last three chapters. It is not always clear, however, where the military command of sexual violence as a strategy comes from, or to prove that the order was given. But in any case, with the creation of a climate within a particular military or paramilitary organisation, in which sexual violence is encouraged or at least tolerated, if not actually ordered, the outcome remains the same for the victims. Moreover, many acts of wartime sexual violence were committed by groups of perpetrators – for example, gang rapes – rather than by individuals. Gang rape may perform a bonding function for groups of men, cementing a sense of loyalty; those who might not rape individually do rape collectively, in a group assertion of masculinity.

In addition, sexual violence against men in episodes of war and ethnic conflict was also both gendered and ethnicised. Rather than being perceived as a homosexual – and thus less masculine – act, male-to-male rape has been often a highly masculinised act for the perpetrator and his audience, asserting power and masculinity, whilst the victim is feminised, reflecting the construction of female sexuality as passive and male sexuality as active. In wartime, male-to-male rape (as male-to-female rape) humiliated and feminised the victim, whilst simultaneously asserting the perpetrator's dominant (heterosexual, ethno-national) masculinity. The ethno-national element means that symbolically, the victim's national identity was also feminised and humiliated. However, although sexual violence against men was prevalent in some cases, it also took forms such as sexual mutilation, castration, sexual humiliation and forcing male prisoners to perform sexual acts upon each other or upon women (often female family members) rather than direct male-to-male rape. Of course, gender is just one variable among others that might be considered, but gender analysis, as Randall has argued, can 'enrich our understanding of genocide and its processes, effects and aftermaths'.[13] For this reason, gender is an important and growing area of research, which has developed our understanding of genocide as a whole, as well as our comprehension of specific cases.

## Genocide Prevention and Intervention

The international system contains significant aspects that have stymied successful attempts at genocide prevention. It is very difficult both to prevent genocide before it starts and to stop it once it has begun. The principle of state sovereignty, which has underpinned the international system since the Treaty of Westphalia (1648), allows individual states to govern their own affairs without the intercession or intervention of outside states.[14] Moreover, the *raison d'être* of the United Nations is to promote international peace, not to undermine state sovereignty. This places it in a very difficult position in terms of dealing with human rights abuses, ethnic cleansing and episodes of genocidal violence, as we have seen many times in recent history. In addition, states always take into account their own interests before considering external events and are motivated by *Realpolitik*.[15] *Realpolitik*, a realistic or pragmatic approach to statesmanship and policy-making (rather than a moral one), therefore plays a significant role in regard to intervention. International norms, policies and mechanisms to prevent and respond to atrocity have been very limited.

The League of Nations, established at the end of the First World War, aimed to create a global system based on diplomacy and the rule of law, seeking to reduce conflict through negotiation and diplomatic means, rather than intervention. However, its members were not prepared to give up any part of their sovereignty in order to achieve its ideals, and so no significant or effective attempts at peacemaking or peacekeeping occurred. At the end of the Second World War, a new international organisation, the United Nations, was created in an effort to improve on the record of its predecessor. New norms were adopted that placed responsibility for human rights violations with individuals. The Nuremberg Principles, adopted by the UN International Law Commission in 1950, stated that every person is responsible for their own deeds and that no individual is outside international law. These principles were later incorporated into the Rome Statute of 1998 – adopted at a conference of 120 states – that subsequently led to the establishment of the International Criminal Court (ICC) in 2002.[16] In 2001, the Canadian government initiated the establishment of the International Commission on Intervention and State Sovereignty (ICISS). This introduced the new concept of the 'Responsibility to Protect' (R2P). A report entitled *The Responsibility to Protect* maintained that the international community has a responsibility both to prevent mass atrocities and to react to crises through a variety of actions, ranging from diplomacy to military intervention. At the UN World Summit in September 2005, heads of state and government endorsed this idea and stated that they were prepared to take timely and decisive collective action in response to states that fail to protect their populations from 'genocide, war crimes, ethnic cleansing and crimes against humanity'. Paragraph 139 states:

We stress the need for the General Assembly to continue consideration of the responsibility to protect populations from genocide, war crimes, ethnic cleansing and crimes against humanity and its implications, bearing in mind the principles of the Charter and international law. We also intend to commit ourselves, as necessary and appropriate, to helping states build capacity to protect their populations from genocide, war crimes, ethnic cleansing and crimes against humanity and to assisting those which are under stress before crises and conflicts break out.

In 2009, the UN Secretary General, Ban Ki-moon put out a new report entitled *Implementing the Responsibility to Protect*. When individual states failed to protect their own populations from genocide, war crimes, ethnic cleansing and crimes against humanity, and only after the international community had attempted to protect such populations through the use of diplomatic, humanitarian and other peaceful means, the signatories to Responsibility to Protect would be authorised to take collective action through the UN Security Council. Since its conception, R2P has become part of the diplomatic currency of international society to prevent and respond to atrocity crimes. However, its concern has centred on 'when and whether to intervene, not how to do so and with what aim in mind'.[17] As Scott Straus notes, the advancement of R2P represents institutional change within the UN system to create a framework for legitimate action to prevent and respond to genocide and mass atrocities.[18]

However, the concept of the responsibility to protect appears hollow in the light of continued war crimes and crimes against humanity affecting populations in armed conflict. The failure to prevent genocides in the twentieth century, as well as war crimes and crimes against humanity, is persisting in the twenty-first century. Despite international laws prohibiting genocide and crimes against humanity, very little has been done to protect the vulnerable victims of such crimes. During the Cold War era, this was mainly because other foreign policy priorities relegated concerns for human rights. But even since the end of the Cold War, the global response to the onset of atrocities has been uneven.[19] The key questions now are these: how can R2P be regarded as a norm and how can mass atrocities be ended? The relationship between human protection and international responsibility and international order, and R2P as 'an established international norm', continue to be contested and not easily resolved.[20] A large community of activists, academics, students and policy-makers grapple with atrocity prevention. Human rights reports expose terrible events across the globe, but neither the UN nor individual governments have stepped in to protect affected populations from such atrocities. UN approval can take a long time or be stymied by the veto of a Security Council permanent member. Guided by *Realpolitik*, most individual sovereign states still consider their own national interests ahead of intervention. *Realpolitik* has meant the lack of a political willingness to intervene to prevent genocide effectively, but there is also a human aspect to this, which is that many politicians and policy-makers have just not cared enough to take decisive action. In addition, in our ever-changing world, factors such as climate change and migration may be the drivers of future atrocities, hence, as Straus advocates: 'As the world changes, so should our approach to atrocity prevention.'[21] The failure of the UN to respond adequately to genocide is described by Adam LeBor, who argues for the possibility of changing how it works in order to make it 'an organization which can prevent and stop genocide'.[22]

The first genocides of the twentieth century did not inspire any major diplomatic efforts to stop the atrocities or to punish the perpetrators. As that century drew to its close in the 1990s, lack of action on the part of the international community in Bosnia and Rwanda made a mockery of the post-Holocaust promise of 'never again'. Many genocide scholars concur: 'Genocide lurks largely in the darkness of irresponsibility and non-accountability, which prevents too little and intervenes too late.'[23] R2P is a signifier of progress towards the possibility of effective atrocity prevention in the international arena. However, as Michael Ignatieff has noted, 'the idea of a responsibility to protect also implies a responsibility to prevent and a responsibility to follow through.'[24] Whether initiatives such as the R2P can succeed over time remains to be seen, but in the meantime, victims trapped in a variety of conflicts remain unaided in their plight. The debate over the use (and overuse) of the term genocide continues to rage among genocide scholars. David Scheffer has proposed that we focus our attention on the prevention of all atrocity crimes, not only genocide, but also war crimes and crimes against humanity. As it is contentious regarding whether or not certain cases constituted genocide, then it is important to work to prevent these crimes whether or not we use the label genocide, which, as we have seen, has a very specific legal definition in international law.[25] Finally, it is worth pointing out that Mamdani takes to task the concept of R2P by stating that it could be 'a clarion call for the recolonization of "failed" states in Africa' and warns against a 'call for justice' as a slogan 'that masks a big power agenda to recolonize Africa'.[26]

## Genocide and Justice

After genocide, the physical and psychological reconstruction of traumatised societies takes place. Bringing to justice the perpetrators is a significant step on the road to recovery for victims who have survived. This section examines briefly some key examples of justice.[27] The trial of key Nazi war criminals at the International Military Tribunal at Nuremberg was, of course, a defining moment in the quest for justice after the Second World War. It began on 20 November

1945, with the intention of punishing leading members of the Nazi government for plunging the world into war and perpetrating war crimes and crimes against humanity. The anger unleashed by the discovery of Nazi mass atrocities was dealt with in a complex yet unwieldy legal process. The main aim of the tribunal was to bring to justice those guilty of planning and waging the Second World War. However, as A. T. Williams has pointed out, there were differences among the victorious Allies in their seeking of justice. They also faced many restrictions and logistical difficulties in their work, including a shortage of personnel. Williams shows too how quickly their fury and disgust dissipated, and how their search for retribution drifted towards indifference. If justice at Nuremberg comprised 'an impersonal and imperfect reaction to human cruelty and human suffering', and was 'symbolic, shambolic, illusory', its attempt to bring justice was nevertheless essential.[28] War crimes and crimes against humanity became increasingly important to investigate, as the news of Nazi atrocities became more widely known. Nuremberg was just one part of the history of the justice meted out by the Allies after 1945. The Nuremberg trials set a precedent for subsequent war crimes trials. The desire to deal with perpetrators of the 'Final Solution' and other crimes against humanity became a significant aspect of post-war justice, with subsequent trials between 1946 and 1949 judging SS members, Nazi doctors and concentration camp commandants. These trials were considered to be a legitimate attempt by the Allied governments to serve justice after the end of the Second World War.[29]

The International Court of Justice (ICJ) was established in 1945 as the main judicial organ of the United Nations, with the aim of settling legal disputes between states.[30] As such, it does not deal with cases pertaining to private individuals or organisations. Only a state can raise a case, and only against another state. For example, in the aftermath of the demise of Yugoslavia in the 1990s, Bosnia and Herzegovina brought a case against Serbia and Montenegro, and Croatia brought a case against Serbia.

The United Nations Security Council established international courts to bring to justice the perpetrators in the former Yugoslavia and in Rwanda. On 25 May 1993, UN Security Council Resolution 827 formally set up the International Criminal Tribunal for the Former

Yugoslavia (ICTY), located in the Hague.[31] This was the first war crimes court established by the United Nations. In trying perpetrators, it aimed to bring justice to victims of the genocide and to deter future would-be perpetrators of genocide. Despite some operational setbacks at the start – including difficulties in the location and detainment of those indicted, as it has no jurisdiction to arrest them in countries that refuse to hand them over – the ICTY has helped to heal some of the wounds inflicted in the region during the 1990s.[32] It has brought charges against many political, military and police leaders – including heads of state – for crimes committed during the break-up of the former Yugoslavia. For example, it brought to trial the former president of Serbia, Slobodan Milošević. He was the first head of state to be tried for genocide.[33] This established a precedent that perpetrators of genocide will face justice if they are indicted and detained. In a very high-profile conviction at the ICTY, in November 2017, Ratko Mladić was sentenced to life imprisonment.

On 9 November 1994, United Nations Security Council Resolution 955 formally established the International Criminal Tribunal for Rwanda (ICTR), located in Arusha in Tanzania.[34] The ICTR brought to trial perpetrators of the Rwandan genocide.[35] In addition to this international tribunal, national chambers were established in Rwanda to bring perpetrators of genocide to justice. Furthermore, the local *gacaca* (community) courts introduced in 2001 dealt with the vast number of Hutu prisoners detained after the genocide. These courts meted out justice and helped to heal Rwandan society. The *gacaca* courts were established because the government determined that 'citizen participation in the search for justice would be critical, not only for the manifestation of the truth about what happened in the genocide, but also to the creation of a conducive environment for the reconciliation of Rwandans'.[36]

In 1997, the Extraordinary Chambers in the Courts of Cambodia was established to bring to trial members of the Khmer Rouge on counts of genocide, war crimes and crimes against humanity. In a prominent case, Kaing Guek Eav, known as Comrade Duch, who was the Director of S–21, was found guilty of crimes against humanity in July 2010 and subsequently sentenced to life imprisonment. There were also other tribunals established to try cases of genocidal crimes in other contexts, such as Bangladesh and Guatemala.[37] The

International Criminal Court, established in 2002 in the Hague, was the first permanent international court. It has strengthened the concept of international justice, as well as the idea that individual perpetrators of genocide and crimes against humanity will no longer be able to act with impunity.[38] There has been debate about the motives and success of all these tribunals. In some instances, they have had a healing effect, but they have also proven divisive and contentious at times, for example, both by those who deny atrocities and by victims and survivors who criticise the distance of their justice. However, prosecutions leading to convictions have had an important impact.

## Memory and Memorialisation

Memory and memorialisation are contested subjects. Some key questions in this context are these: What purpose does memory serve? How does the way that historical events are remembered serve particular groups or agendas? In terms of memorials, how is it possible to represent these events accurately or appropriately in stone? Processes of memorialisation and commemoration are significant to our understanding of genocides. States or communities set into stone their own distinct narratives or tell their own stories or the ones they want to be told and remembered. By its nature, this short section cannot provide a comprehensive coverage of all genocide memorials and museums. It begins with a discussion of Holocaust memory and memorialisation, followed by an indication of how some of the other genocides discussed in this book have been memorialised and remembered.

In an era in which memory has become so important, commemorating genocide, and the Holocaust in particular, has become a significant part of our popular consciousness. David MacDonald describes the 'searing impact on Western consciousness' of the Holocaust.[39] This and other genocides have been represented in a variety of ways, including art forms, literature and film.[40] These too have added to the way in which these events have become part of popular knowledge and memory. Memorials, museums and commemorative events have become a salient part of popular understanding of the Holocaust and other genocides, as well as a means of education for the prevention of future atrocities. Memorialisation of the Holocaust and other genocides guides popular emotions. Alon Confino contends that memorialisation should 'become a socio-cultural mode of action'.[41] Collective memory can act as a compensation for loss and as a marker of stability in uncertain times.[42] Popular memory is different from the memories of those who experienced the event, although, of course, the survivors of genocides have helped to shape it through their testimonies and narratives.

After the occurrence of an event so momentous in history that it called into question the self-assurance of Western civilisation, what form of monument could commemorate the Holocaust? Dan Stone has noted how 'varied, complex, and hotly debated' Holocaust memorialisation has proven to be.[43] There has been a division between those seeking to incorporate the Holocaust into traditional forms of commemoration, such as easily recognisable statues, narrative museums and formal commemorative events following conventional patterns, and those looking for ways of commemoration that in themselves embody the fundamental uneasiness of possibility of Holocaust commemoration, such as 'counter-monuments', memorials and sites requiring input from visitors and disorientating architecture.

James Young contends: 'An appropriate memorial design will acknowledge the void left behind and not concentrate on the memory of terror and destruction alone.'[44] Early Holocaust commemoration took the form of mass personal memory, with those who survived the Holocaust involved in the process of memorialisation, such as the Warsaw Ghetto monument, unveiled in 1948. One side of this monument represents disaster; the other side portrays heroism, marking the uprising in April 1943. In the Cold War era, creators of memorials in Eastern European countries behind the Iron Curtain faced constraints posed by Communist doctrine. Memorials had to satisfy Stalinist ideology, which maintained that all social conflicts had at their core the issue of class division. This meant that the memorialisation of the Holocaust as the mass murder of the Jews was challenging to convey. Communist ideology believed that anti-Semitism was a tool used by 'the bosses' of Nazism to steer 'the masses' away from recognising their real class interests. In addition, identifying different victim groups contradicted the myth that all victims of Nazism were fighters for the new society to be brought about by communism. There were some attempts by historians to discuss the fate of Jews as separate from that of the Red Army, the Soviet population as a whole, or the communist partisans, but this was rare. The 1959 monument to commemorate the massacre of 35,000 Jews at Babi Yar exemplified this trend, as it contained no mention of Jews. The 1967 memorial at Auschwitz too mentions only the '4 million people' who 'suffered and died here at the hands of the Nazi murderers', but does not refer to the Jews.[45] Thus this lack of specific mention of Jews as victims of National Socialism in post-war communist collective memory was part of a broader smoothing over of memory in the communist states that disregarded the complexity of difference, in order to put forward the representation of heroic communist resistance against fascism and Nazism.

Communist doctrine portrayed a particular version of events in such memorials that told the specific story that accorded with its aims and agenda. These remained in place throughout the Cold War era, only changing after the fall of the USSR. Many small memorials erected by the few local Jews still remaining in Eastern Europe were a brave attempt to challenge this official communist line of memory, which disregarded the complexities of what had occurred during the Second World War. During the Cold War era, Western portrayals also put forward their own heroic, national narratives. These depictions not only overlooked the reality of widespread collaboration with Nazism across Europe, but also extinguished differences between victim groups. They were designed to assist in the process of national reconstruction. The representation of Jewish or Sinti and Roma victims was often considered to be less important than that of those 'national heroes' who took part in anti-Nazi resistance.

Therefore, it took until several decades after the end of the Second World War for proper Holocaust memorialisation to emerge. Before that, only the first institutions that were set up to record the experience of Jews during the war – such as YIVO in New York, the Wiener Library in London and the Jewish Historical Institute in Warsaw – acted as repositories for collective memory. It was only in the 1970s and 1980s that an interest in commemorating the

Holocaust and building Holocaust memorials developed in Western Europe, Israel and the USA. To be sure, there were heated debates about how these should be created. Were traditional statues and types of memorials suitable to represent the Holocaust? Should the focus be on suffering alone? In West Germany, how would memorials be constructed in the land of the perpetrators?

Many artists subverted traditional meanings of memorials, creating objects and places that confronted visitors with the challenge of being forced to consider their own involvement in the 'memory-work' or counter-monuments. Young describes these as 'self-conscious memorial spaces conceived to challenge the very premises of their being'.[46] These are not places for calm contemplation, but for confronting the past. For example, the Monument against Fascism in Hamburg – created by Jochen Gerz and Esther Shalev-Gerz – was a forty-foot high lead column on which people wrote messages.[47] The monument was gradually lowered into the ground, until it disappeared in 1993. This, as well as numerous other counter-monuments, demands interaction. As Young notes, they are designed 'not to console but to provoke'.[48] Berlin's Central Monument to the Murdered Jews of Europe – the field of stelae, designed by Peter Eisenman – created considerable controversy. Critics argued that such a massive central monument in the heart of Berlin would be an attempt to close off this chapter of history and that it could not account for the varied and complex nature of the Holocaust experience. Advocates regarded it as a proper representation of Germany's attempts to deal with its Nazi past and maintained that its size and position would not allow that past to be forgotten. As Stone notes: 'The evocation of the incomplete always leaves space for renewed questioning, in ways that traditional forms of monumentalization – which insist on closure and continuity – do not.'[49] Daniel Libeskind's Jewish Museum, with its disorientating architecture, and Berlin's Central Monument to the Murdered Jews of Europe both exemplify this intention of perpetual interrogation rather than passivity of memory.

*Stolpersteine* (stumbling stones) have been a controversial method of Holocaust commemoration. Starting in the late 1990s, German artist Gunter Demnig initiated a project to situate 'stumbling stones' outside the homes of Holocaust victims. Brass plates, the size of cobblestones, have been placed into the pavements, indicating the names of the victims as a means of keeping their memory alive, as advocates of the project have stated. However, there have been voices of dissent, claiming that victims deserve better than such plaques in the pavement, easily covered with dust and dirt. By now, tens of thousands of stumbling stones have been placed in many European countries where Jews had lived before the 'Final Solution'. These stones state the name of the victims, the date and destination of deportation and the date of death, where these details are known.

Furthermore, the Nazi concentration camps and death camps have become sites of memory, as well as of education. Museums too, including Yad Vashem in Jerusalem, founded in 1953, the Imperial War Museum in London and the United States Holocaust Memorial Museum in Washington DC, have a crucial part to play in both the preservation of memory and education.[50] Andreas Huyssen notes that museums do not simply represent the past, but are also 'sites of cultural contestation and negotiation'.[51] Curators have faced numerous challenges in their conceptions of Holocaust exhibitions and museums, as well as museums and exhibitions that treat the theme of genocide more generally, such as the Museum of Tolerance and Memory in Mexico City, which was founded in 1999 – for example, which victims to represent and why; how to portray the perpetrators; the distinction between private and public memory; how to direct (or not direct) visitors' thoughts; what aspects of the history are being told or left untold; how much tension to create through use of space; which artefacts to select.

Memorial days, which represent an obvious way to commemorate and mark past events, can also pose difficulties and controversies. How is it best to design them? Who are they for? Whose story do they tell and whose story do they omit? In drawing attention to a range of genocides, such events can have an important educational impact. For example, Britain's first annual Holocaust Memorial Day was held in January 2001.[52] An event commemorating the Srebrenica massacre of July 1995 is also held annually on 11 July each year.

The Armenian Genocide Memorial at Tsitsernakaberd in Yerevan, Armenia was constructed in 1967 (see Figure 9). It is formed of a forty-four-metre stela, with twelve inclined granite slabs forming a circle that surrounds an eternal flame. A ceremony to mark the anniversary of the genocide is held here annually on 24 April: the

**FIGURE 9** *Armenian Genocide Memorial, at Yerevan, Armenia.*

Armenian Genocide Remembrance Day. In addition, there are Armenian genocide memorials in different countries, especially the USA, where diasporic communities have represented and commemorated the genocide. Memories of loss and exile have haunted new generations and had a profound effect on the identity of Armenians who have assimilated narratives of their national suffering more than a century ago.

In Cambodia, Tuol Sleng is now a museum that educates visitors about the genocide under the Khmer Rouge.[53] At the killing fields of Choeung Ek, a memorial was established in 1988 in order to house the remains of nearly 9,000 victims that were discovered at mass gravesites there. The Choeung Ek Memorial has a display of exhumed human remains, evidencing the mass murders perpetrated by the Khmer Rouge. Furthermore, many local memorials throughout Cambodia mark the sites of former Khmer Rouge mass graves.[54] Local or regional authorities constructed memorials during the 1980s, and some have been rebuilt in the interim too. They have provided a public space for the remains of victims and a location where religious ceremonies could be performed. These memorials stand in places where victims were imprisoned, executed or buried. The Khmer Rouge often used temple compounds for imprisonment and mass interment, and so memorials have often been placed inside or near to temples. For example, two shrines have been dedicated to victims of the Khmer Rouge at Wat Phnom Sampeou at Battambang.

As Rachel Hughes notes: 'Cambodia's genocide memorials are products of contestations between multiple actors, meanings and values, including Cambodian party-politics, Khmer Buddhist beliefs about death, and local and internationalised discourses of justice, education and memory.'[55] In addition, James Tyner's examination of the ongoing memorialisation of violence in Cambodia shows how a legacy of organised mass violence has become part of a cultural heritage and how this heritage is 'produced'.[56] Tyner contends that the selective memorialisation of Cambodia's violent past under the Khmer Rouge negates the everyday lived experiences of millions of Cambodians and diminishes the efforts to bring about social justice and reconciliation. And so, once again, we see here the impact of political agendas and the controversial nature of memorials.

In Bosnia, the Srebrenica Genocide Memorial comprises the memorial-cemetery complex Srebrenica-Potočari, which honours and commemorates the victims of the genocide. In 2015, it launched a virtual museum, which allows people from across the world to 'virtually' visit the Memorial Centre. They can enter the gates of the Memorial Centre and begin a virtual tour, reading the names of victims on the Memorial Wall and exploring the grounds and the museum.

Rwanda faced a massive multifaceted task of reconstruction, restitution, recovery and reconciliation in the aftermath of the genocide of 1994. Memorialisation formed a part of this complex process. A number of memorial sites in Rwanda commemorate the events of 1994, and 7 April has been designated as the annual day of remembrance of the victims of the Rwandan genocide. The Kigali Genocide Memorial Centre, which opened in April 2004, is perhaps the most well-known and is the final resting place for more than 250,000 victims of the genocide, as well as an important exhibition centre. But this is just one of many memorial sites across the country. Others include the memorials at key locations where mass slaughters took place – for example, at Murambi, Gisenyi, Nyamata, Nyanza,

Bisesero, Nyarubuye and Ntarama. The mass murders often occurred at churches and convents, where victims had come to seek refuge, and at schools and other compounds. Memorials and/or cemeteries, exhibitions and displays have been established at these locations to commemorate the victims of the genocide.

When we think about the memorialisation of genocides, locations such as the Auschwitz-Birkenau Memorial and State Museum in Poland, Yad Vashem in Israel, the Srebrenica-Potočari Cemetery in Bosnia and the Kigali Genocide Memorial Centre in Rwanda come to mind. These places are permanent, physical reminders of genocide. They are also focal points for large-scale remembrance ceremonies, and therefore part of the process and development of the collective memory of the events that occurred. When memorialisation is carried out with care and sensitivity, it can play a significant role in helping to heal societies, but when it is not, it can be divisive and reinforce distinctions of perpetrators and victims, exacerbating divisions between communities. Memorials and the creation of memory are highly contested for a variety of reasons. Thus certain aspects of memorialisation processes can raise difficult and uncomfortable issues, as well as heated controversies. Many memorials have been erected that put forward a specific version of events or tell a particular story that is not the entire story. Although the concepts and contexts of memory and memorialisation are challenging and pose numerous areas for contention and debate, on balance, it is better to persist with efforts to uphold memories and to commemorate these events – even if such attempts have shortcomings – than to let the events be forgotten.

## Questions for Further Discussion

1   Why does gender matter in a discussion of genocide?

2   How have discourses about masculinity contributed to the transformation of ordinary men into killers?

3   What dilemmas do genocide prevention and intervention present to individual sovereign states and to the United Nations?

**4** How have measures designed to prevent genocide and mass atrocities developed over the course of the twentieth and the start of the twenty-first centuries?

**5** Why is memorialisation often such a contested matter?

# Further Reading

Bellamy, A. and Dunne, T., *The Oxford Handbook of the Responsibility to Protect* (Oxford, 2016).

Bosco, D., *Rough Justice: The International Criminal Court in a World of Power Politics* (New York and Oxford, 2014).

Corey, D. and Beezley, W. (eds), *Genocide, Collective Violence, and Popular Memory: The Politics of Remembrance in the Twentieth Century* (Wilmington, DE, 2002).

Jinks, R., *Representing Genocide: The Holocaust as Paradigm* (London, 2016).

Jones, A. (ed.), *Gendercide and Genocide* (Nashville, TN, 2004).

MacDonald, D., *Identity Politics in the Age of Genocide: The Holocaust and Historical Representation* (London and New York, 2008).

Randall, A. (ed.), *Genocide and Gender in the Twentieth Century* (London, 2015).

Rittner, C. and Roth, J. (eds), *Rape: Weapon of War and Genocide* (St. Paul, MN, 2012).

Rittner, C., Roth, J. and Smith, J. (eds), *Will Genocide Ever End?* (St. Paul, MN, 2002).

Schabas, W., *An Introduction to the International Criminal Court* (Cambridge, 2011).

Sharples, C. and Jensen, O. (eds), *Britain and the Holocaust: Remembering and Representing War and Genocide* (Basingstoke, 2013).

Straus, S., *Fundamentals of Genocide and Mass Atrocity Prevention* (Washington, DC, 2016).

Waller, J., *Confronting Evil. Engaging our Responsibility to Prevent Genocide* (Oxford, 2016).

Young, J., *At Memory's Edge: After-Images of the Holocaust in Contemporary Art and Architecture* (New Haven, CT, 2000).

but also of victims, bystanders, collaborators and resisters. Why do people react in the ways that they do?

The varied and substantial scholarship about genocide, across a gamut of academic disciplines, has made it a topic rife with debate. Why do such differences in interpretations exist? We do not necessarily or easily reach the final or definitive answers in our study and discussion. This field is extremely fast growing and will continue to evolve. The debates and areas of interest will inevitably change over time. New areas of exploration and investigation will develop and the scholarly literature will move on. For example, we have seen how recent developments have explored ecological factors and climate change and their relationship to genocide, shifting the paradigm and suggesting new areas of concern for the future. Recent additions to the academic literature written from the perspective of gender have also changed and advanced the field of genocide studies.

Although much of the focus of this book has been on the twentieth century – often referred to in the scholarly literature as the 'century of genocide' – it began with an analysis of earlier examples of colonial genocide. It considered links between the processes of colonialism and genocide. Whilst there were cases in which there was a clear, causal link between the two historical processes, it is erroneous to conflate centuries of colonial history in a singular manner. Certainly, a backdrop of expansionist and racist ideas informed colonialism, particularly in the late nineteenth century. However, not all the outcomes of the colonial project were the same. It is necessary to distinguish between different examples in order to establish the links between colonialism and genocide as two significant historical processes. To be sure, settler colonialism resulted in the removal or destruction of pre-existing indigenous populations. However, there were huge variations in the history of colonialism across the globe and across several centuries. The problem with applying the UN definition of genocide to colonial cases of mass death is that most of the depopulation was not usually the direct result of policies intended at extermination or annihilation. The main reason for catastrophic population decline, in Australia and the Americas, as we have seen, was disease, an unintended effect of European settler colonialism, as well as other factors such as malnutrition, alcohol and increased intertribal warfare. And yet there were also, as we have noted, intentional policies aimed at the eradication of native populations. In the end, then, we should take care when using the term genocide in the context of colonialism, not to use it ubiquitously, but to apply it to specific examples of intentional massacres of peoples based on their belonging to membership of a particular group – such as policies towards the Yana and the Tolowa tribes in North America, or those towards Aboriginal peoples in Queensland in Australia in the second half of the nineteenth century, or those of the German Empire towards the Herero in German South West Africa – rather than labelling all colonial policy as genocide.

Moving into the twentieth century, we saw that the Armenian genocide resulted, in part, from religious, linguistic and cultural differences between the Armenians and the Turks that had created strains and conflicts at times between these two communities over many centuries. The tensions between the Turks and the Armenians had increased significantly during the course of the late nineteenth century, in particular as the Ottoman Empire came under threat. However, it was the rise to power of the Young Turks, with their vehemently nationalist, exclusivist Turkic ideology, that precipitated the greatest catastrophe for the Armenian population. The Young Turks perceived the Armenians as threatening and inimical to the state. In the context of the First World War, they were able to mobilise state power and the military against the Armenians, leading to their deportation and mass murder. The destruction of Armenian churches and buildings signified the intention of the Young Turk regime to eliminate all remnants of the cultural heritage of the Armenians and indeed any memory of their existence in this region. The planning, coordination, scale and implementation of this killing project by the CUP made it a classic case of genocide.

The Nazi regime was responsible for two separate genocides that occurred more or less simultaneously during the Second World War. The first was the 'Final Solution', the mass murder of European Jews. The responsibility for the 'Final Solution' extended far beyond Hitler himself – we have noted the roles of Goering, Heydrich and Himmler, among other key Nazi leaders, the *SS-Einsatzgruppen*, the *Gauleiter*, even civil servants. It is necessary to take into account all the people and organisations involved in the transportation and the killing of the Jews of Europe at the death camps – from the provision of a vast network of railway transportation to the chemical company that produced the Zyklon B for the gas chambers, as well as many others that organised and ran the Nazi camps. Complicity also extends, as we have seen, to the many ordinary people who stood to gain from the economic plunder of Jewish assets and possessions, not only in Germany but across many European lands including Austria, Poland, Hungary and Romania. In the end, through the use of mass shootings and death camps, the Nazis' 'Final Solution', carried out as a pan-European project of genocide, took the lives of some 6 million European Jews. The second Nazi genocide was that of the Sinti and Roma ('Gypsies') – the *Porrajmos*. It is difficult to be certain of the total number of 'Gypsies' who were murdered by the Nazis. This is partly because of the erratic methods used to capture and murder the 'Gypsies' and because 'Gypsy' prisoners were not a high priority to the Nazis. In addition, few accurate records were kept of their deaths. Many of the massacres of 'Gypsies' in Eastern and Southern Europe, which occurred at numerous sites in fields and forests, were not recorded. Furthermore, most 'Gypsy' families were killed in their entirety, leaving no survivors to detail the number of dead. Estimates of the number of Sinti and Roma who perished in the *Porrajmos* vary from 250,000 to over 1 million. The Sinti and Roma remained the forgotten victims of Nazi genocide for many decades.

In Cambodia, between 1975 and 1979, the Khmer Rouge regime mercilessly targeted and massacred a very significant proportion of Cambodia's population during the course of its communist revolution. The victims of the Khmer Rouge were ethnically and religiously motivated in many cases. In particular, the eradication of the Buddhist monks and the Muslim Chams on grounds of their religion, and the Vietnamese and the Chinese on grounds of their ethnicity, is illustrative of this. In other cases, policies directed against urban people, intellectuals or 'enemies' of the regime were largely politically motivated. The Khmer Rouge put into place a nationwide system of terror through imprisonment, interrogation, torture and execution. In the final analysis, all of the victims of the regime were murdered because they were considered to be undesirable or impure, whether on ethnic, religious or political grounds. Mass gravesites across Cambodia testify to the wholesale massacres of both ethnic and religious groups, as well as political opponents. The revolutionary ideology of the Pol Pot regime resulted in the annihilation of an estimated 1.7–2 million people between 1975 and 1979. The decade of the 1990s witnessed two large-scale episodes of genocide: one in the former Yugoslavia and the other in Rwanda. The wars of Yugoslavian secession in the 1990s were not motivated entirely by ancient hatred. Economic instability in the 1980s had been accompanied by the rise of nationalism after Tito's death, and in particular, the deliberate revival and exploitation of painful historical memories from the Second World War by nationalist leaders. Milošević's ardent nationalism included a sense of displeasure and resentment over previous injustices perpetrated against the Serbs, from Kosovo Polje (1389) to the Jasenovac concentration camp in the Second World War, where Croatians had massacred Serbs, as well as Jews and 'Gypsies'. Milošević's nationalism was redemptive, aiming to bring together the dispersed Serbian population into a greater Serbia and to restore the Serb nation to greatness and glory. Milošević employed propaganda effectively to inflame tensions between the Serbs and the other ethnic groups in the region, and used military force to bring about his desire to homogenise territory and recast it for his own goals. The intention of Serb (and indeed Croat) nationalists in Bosnia, in particular, was to define categorically who was Serb, who was Croat and who was Muslim, and to determine people's fates based upon this definition. The death toll in Bosnia is estimated at 100,000, with 8,372 Muslim males killed alone at the Srebrenica massacre in July 1995.

In 1994, the genocide that occurred in Rwanda was fast and brutal. This was not a spontaneous, chaotic and disorderly action; on the contrary, it was carefully planned and organised, using the apparatus of the state and the media, to carry out and promote the mass murder of the Tutsi. The unwillingness of the international political community to intervene in Rwanda meant that the Hutu perpetrators had not only the motives and means, but also the opportunity to execute their genocidal plans. The extent of popular participation and the speed with which the mass murder of the Tutsi minority took place are among the most noteworthy and distinctive characteristics of the Rwandan genocide. The genocide in Rwanda was a paradigmatic case, crucial to the field of genocide studies.

At the start of the twenty-first century, the genocide of the Fur, Massalit and Zaghawa peoples in the Darfur region of Sudan took place. This was another significant episode that illuminated an array of issues, including tensions between different groups, counterinsurgency, ethnic cleansing, the impact of climactic change in the region on competition for land and resources, as well as the contentious question of the response of the rest of the world. As Mahmood Mamdani notes about the semantics, there is a tendency to be permissive of insurgency or liberation war, counterinsurgency (the suppression of civil war, or rebel/revolutionary movements) and interstate war as integral to the exercise of national sovereignty, whilst condemnation is reserved for genocide. Definitions remain a thorny issue among genocide scholars in a variety of disciplines and more widely in the media and society. An understanding of debates over definitions and criteria is crucial to a proper comprehension of this complex topic.

What challenges are involved in linking genocide to other large historical events such as the collapse of empires, colonialism, war and civil war? We have looked at cases in which there is a clear link between genocide and civil war, but civil war does not mean a war against civilians. Some civil wars become genocidal, but not all. We have considered genocide during major global conflicts (the Armenians during the First World War and the Jews and the Sinti and Roma during the Second World War). We have noted the implications of race and of nation-building and state-building on genocide, as well as the motivations of plunder and pillaging in terms of complicity and popular participation, particularly in the Holocaust and in the Rwandan genocide. There are many areas for further study and debate that are just not possible to include in a book of this nature and length. Some of these are posed in the final set of questions for further discussion below.

Let us end with the words of two Holocaust survivors who wrote down their testimonies for particular reasons. Primo Levi, an Italian survivor of Auschwitz, was determined to survive in order to bear witness. He commented on the aim of the Nazi camps to 'reduce us to beasts'. But, he wrote:

we must not become beasts; that even in this place one can survive, and therefore one must want to survive, to tell the story, to bear witness; and that to survive we must force ourselves to save at least the skeleton, the scaffolding, the form of civilization.[1]

Livia Bitton-Jackson, who grew up in Hungary before being deported to Poland, set down her experiences at Auschwitz, published in 1999, in order to help new and future generations to learn from the past:

> My hope is that learning about past evils will help us to avoid them in the future. My hope is that learning what horrors can result from prejudice and intolerance, we can cultivate a commitment to fight prejudice and intolerance. It is for this reason that I wrote my recollections of the horror . . . My stories are of gas chambers, shootings, electrified fences, torture, scorching sun, mental abuse, and constant threat of death. But they are also stories of faith, hope, triumph and love . . . My story is my message. Never give up.[2]

## Questions for Further Discussion

1 How do genocides end?

2 What are the outcomes of genocides for societies that experience them?

3 How adequate has restitution and compensation been for surviving victims of genocide?

4 What are 'subaltern' genocides?

5 How have the Holocaust and other genocides been represented in films, novels and other genres beyond academia?

# Notes

## Introduction: The Concept of Genocide and its Definition

1 L. Kuper, *Genocide: Its Political Use in the Twentieth Century* (Harmondsworth, 1981), p. 9.

2 R. Lemkin, *Axis Rule in Occupied Europe: Laws of Occupation, Analysis of Government, Proposals for Redress* (Washington, DC, 1944).

3 Cited in A. Jones, *Genocide: A Comprehensive Introduction* (Oxford and New York, 2017), p. 15.

4 For detailed scholarly analysis of this, see J. Quigley, *The Genocide Convention: An International Law Analysis* (Farnham, 2006) and H. van der Wilt, J. Vervliet, G. Sluiter and J. ten Cate (eds), *The Genocide Convention: The Legacy of 60 Years* (Leiden and Boston, 2012).

5 F. Chalk and K. Jonassohn, *The History and Sociology of Genocide: Analyses and Case Studies* (New Haven, CT and London, 1990), p. 23.

6 B. Harff, 'Genocide as State Terrorism', in M. Stohl and G. Lopez (eds), *Government Violence and Repression* (New York, 1986), p. 165.

7 G. Heinsohn, 'What Makes the Holocaust a Uniquely Unique Genocide?', *Journal of Genocide Research* Vol. 2, No. 3 (2000), pp. 411–30.

8 A. Dirk Moses, 'The Holocaust and Genocide', in D. Stone (ed.), *Historiography of the Holocaust* (Basingstoke, 2004), p. 535.

9 H. Huttenbach, 'Locating the Holocaust on the Genocide Spectrum', *Holocaust and Genocide Studies* Vol. 3, No. 3 (1988), pp. 289–303. See also M. Levene, 'Is the Holocaust Simply Another Example of Genocide?', *Patterns of Prejudice* Vol. 28, No. 2 (1994), pp. 3–26 and A. Rosenbaum (ed.), *Is the Holocaust Unique?* (Boulder, CO, 2001).

10 W. Churchill, *A Little Matter of Genocide: Holocaust and Denial in the Americas 1492 to the Present* (San Francisco, 1997) and D. Stannard, *American Holocaust: The Conquest of the New World*

(Oxford, 1992). On this subject, see also A. Alvarez, *Native America and the Question of Genocide* (Lanham, 2016).

**11**  D. Moshman, 'Conceptual Constraints on Thinking about Genocide', *Journal of Genocide Research* Vol. 3, No. 3 (2001), p. 432.

**12**  C. Gerlach, *Extremely Violent Societies: Mass Violence in the Twentieth Century World* (Cambridge, 2010) and B. Valentino, *Final Solutions: Mass Killing and Genocide in the Twentieth Century* (Ithaca, NY, 2004).

**13**  D. Bloxham, 'The Armenian Genocide of 1915–16: Cumulative Radicalization and the Development of a Destruction Policy', *Past and Present* Vol. 181, No. 1 (2003), p. 189.

**14**  Ibid.

**15**  C. Anderton and J. Brauer (eds), *Economic Aspects of Genocides, Other Mass Atrocities, and Their Prevention* (Oxford, 2016); D. Armitage, *Civil Wars: A History in Ideas* (New Haven, CT and London, 2017).

**16**  J. Waller, *Becoming Evil: How Ordinary People Commit Genocide and Mass Murder* (Oxford, 2007).

**17**  M. Jasinski, *Examining Genocides: Means, Motive, and Opportunity* (London and New York, 2017), p. 7.

**18**  D. Short, *Redefining Genocide: Settler Colonialism, Social Death and Ecocide* (London, 2016), pp. 5 and 6.

**19**  Ibid., pp. 8–9.

**20**  A. Alvarez, *Unstable Ground: Climate Change, Conflict, and Genocide* (Lanham, 2017), p. 3.

**21**  Ibid., p. 141.

# 1: Colonial Genocides

**1**  See M. Turda and M. S. Quine, *Historicizing Race* (London, 2018), pp. 33–48.

**2**  On this, see P. Wolfe, 'Settler Colonialism and the Elimination of the Native', *Journal of Genocide Research* Vol. 8, No. 4 (2006), pp. 387–409 and J. Docker, 'Are Settler-Colonies Inherently Genocidal? Re-reading Lemkin', in A. Dirk Moses (ed.), *Empire, Colony, Genocide: Conquest, Occupation, and Subaltern Resistance in World History* (New York, 2010), pp. 81–101.

**3**  E. Barkan, 'Genocides of Indigenous Peoples: Rhetoric of Human Rights', in R. Gellately and B. Kiernan (eds), *The Specter of Genocide: Mass Murder in Historical Perspectives* (Cambridge, 2003), p. 118.

**4** W. Churchill, *A Little Matter of Genocide: Holocaust and Denial in the Americas 1492 to the Present* (San Francisco, 1997) and D. Stannard, *American Holocaust: The Conquest of the New World* (New York, 1992). For a useful summary of the historiography, see A. Cave, 'Genocide in the Americas', in D. Stone (ed.), *The Historiography of Genocide* (Basingstoke, 2010), pp. 273–95.

**5** G. Tinker, *Missionary Conquest: The Gospel and Native American Cultural Genocide* (Boston, MA, 1993), p. 4.

**6** D. Short, *Redefining Genocide: Settler Colonialism, Social Death and Ecocide* (London, 2016), p. 36.

**7** For example, see S. Stanton, 'Time for Truth: Speaking the Unspeakable – Genocide and Apartheid in the "Lucky" Country', *Australian Humanities Review*, July 1999. For a useful summary of the historiography, see T. Barta, 'Decent Disposal: Australian Historians and the Recovery of Genocide', in Stone (ed.), *The Historiography of Genocide*, pp. 296–322.

**8** On this, see R. Van Krieken, 'The Barbarism of Civilization: Cultural Genocide and the "Stolen Generation"', *British Journal of Sociology* Vol. 50, No. 2 (1999), pp. 297–315; R. Van Krieken, 'Rethinking Cultural Genocide: Aboriginal Child Removal and Settler-colonial State Formation', *Oceania* Vol. 75, No. 2 (2004), pp. 125–51; and R. Van Krieken, 'Cultural Genocide', in Stone (ed.), *The Historiography of Genocide*, pp. 128–55.

**9** On this, see M. Gordon, 'Colonial Violence and Holocaust Studies', *Holocaust Studies: A Journal of Culture and History* Vol. 21, No. 4 (2015), pp. 272–91. See also M. Hawkins, *Social Darwinism in European and American Thought: Nature as Model and Nature as Threat* (Cambridge, 1997).

**10** A. Alvarez, *Native America and the Question of Genocide* (Lanham, MD, 2016), p. 139.

**11** B. Madley, 'The Genocide of California's Yana Indians', in S. Totten and W. Parsons (eds), *Centuries of Genocide: Essays and Eyewitness Accounts* (New York, 2012), pp. 16–53.

**12** B. Madley, 'When "The World Was Turned Upside Down": California and Oregon's Tolowa Indian Genocide, 1851–1856', in A. Jones (ed.), *New Directions in Genocide Research* (New York, 2012), p. 171.

**13** Ibid., p. 191.

**14** B. Madley, 'Reexamining the American Genocide Debate: Meaning, Historiography, and New Methods', *American Historical Review* Vol. 120, No. 1 (2015), pp. 98–139.

**15** On this, see J. Milloy, *A National Crime: The Canadian Government and the Residential School System, 1879–1986* (Winnipeg, 1999) and A. Woolford, *This Benevolent Experiment: Indigenous Boarding Schools, Genocide, and Redress in Canada and the United States* (Winnipeg, 2015).

16  N. Ascherson, *The King Incorporated: Leopold the Second and the Congo* (London, 1999), p. 9.

17  A. Hochschild, *King Leopold's Ghost* (Boston, MA, 1998), p. 233.

18  E. Weitz, *A Century of Genocide: Utopias of Race and Nation* (Princeton, NJ and Oxford, 2003), p. 46.

19  B. Kiernan, *Blood and Soil: A World History of Genocide and Extermination from Sparta to Darfur* (New Haven, CT and London, 2007), p. 38.

20  Ascherson, *The King Incorporated*, p. 9.

21  On this, see J. Bridgman, *The Revolt of the Hereros* (Berkeley and Los Angeles, CA, 1981).

22  J. Bridgman and L. Worley, 'Genocide of the Hereros', in S. Totten and W. Parsons (eds), *Century of Genocide: Critical Essays and Eyewitness Accounts* (New York and London, 2009), p. 18.

23  I. Hull, 'Military Culture and the Production of "Final Solutions" in the Colonies: The Example of Wilhelminian Germany', in R. Gellately and B. Kiernan (eds), *The Specter of Genocide* (Cambridge, 2003), p. 142.

24  J. Sarkin, *Germany's Genocide of the Herero: Kaiser Wilhelm II, His General, His Settlers, His Soldiers* (Cape Town, 2010), p. 244. See also J. Swan, 'The Final Solution in South West Africa', *Quarterly Journal of Military History* Vol. 3, No. 4 (1991), pp. 36–55.

25  On this, see, for example, Hull, 'Military Culture and the Production of "Final Solutions" in the Colonies', pp. 141–62; J. Zimmerer, 'The Birth of the *Ostland* out of the Spirit of Colonialism: A Postcolonial Perspective on the Nazi Policy of Conquest and Extermination', *Patterns of Prejudice* Vol. 39, No. 2 (2005), pp. 197–219; J. Zimmerer, 'Colonial Genocide: The Herero and Nama War (1904–8) in German South West Africa and Its Significance', in Stone (ed.), *The Historiography of Genocide*, pp. 323–43; and B. Madley, 'From Africa to Auschwitz: How German South West Africa Incubated Ideas and Methods Adopted and Developed by the Nazis in Eastern Europe', *European History Quarterly* Vol. 35, No. 3 (2005), pp. 429–64.

26  Hull, 'Military Culture and the Production of "Final Solutions" in the Colonies', p. 142.

27  Sarkin, *Germany's Genocide of the Herero*, p. 244.

28  On this, see A. Dirk Moses (ed.), *Genocide and Settler Society: Frontier Violence and Stolen Indigenous Children in Australian*

*History* (Oxford, 2004). See also, C. Tatz, 'Genocide in Australia', *Journal of Genocide Research* Vol. 1, No. 3 (1999), pp. 315–52.

29  A. Dirk Moses, 'An Antipodean Genocide? The Origins of the Genocidal Moment in the Colonization of Australia', *Journal of Genocide Research* Vol. 2, No. 1 (2000), p. 90.

30  N. Clements, *The Black War: Fear, Sex and Resistance in Tasmania* (St Lucia, Queensland, 2014).

31  On this, see L. Ryan, *The Aboriginal Tasmanians* (St Lucia, Queensland, 1981); H. Reynolds, *An Indelible Stain? The Question of Genocide in Australia's History* (Melbourne, 2001); H. Reynolds, *A Forgotten War* (Sydney, 2013); A. Curthoys, 'Genocide in Tasmania: The History of an Idea', in A. Dirk Moses (ed.), *Empire, Colony, Genocide: Conquest, Occupation, and Subaltern Resistance in World History* (New York, 2010), pp. 229–52; T. Lawson, *The Last Man: A British Genocide in Tasmania* (London, 2014).

32  Curthoys, 'Genocide in Tasmania: The History of an Idea', p. 246.

33  Wolfe, 'Settler Colonialism and the Elimination of the Native', p. 387.

34  P. Brantlinger, *Dark Vanishings: Discourse on the Extinction of Primitive Races, 1800–1930* (Ithaca, NY, 2001).

## 2: The Armenian Genocide

1  A useful summary of this discourse may be found in D. Bloxham and F. Göçek, 'The Armenian Genocide', in D. Stone (ed.), *The Historiography of Genocide* (Basingstoke, 2010), pp. 344–72, especially pp. 344–55.

2  D. Bloxham, 'The Armenian Genocide of 1915–1916: Cumulative Radicalization and the Development of a Destruction Policy', *Past and Present* Vol. 181, No. 1 (2003), p. 143.

3  R. Kévorkian, *The Armenian Genocide: A Complete History* (London, 2011), p. 1.

4  U. Üngör, 'Fresh Understandings of the Armenian Genocide', in A. Jones (ed.), *New Directions in Genocide Research* (London and New York, 2012), p. 199. The Matryoshka doll or Russian doll is the set of wooden dolls of decreasing sizes placed inside each other.

5  V. Dadrian, *Warrant for Genocide: Key Elements of the Turko-Armenian Conflict* (New Brunswick, NJ and London, 2006), p. 165.

6  M. Wyszomirski, 'Communal Violence: The Armenians and the Copts as Case Studies', *World Politics* Vol. 27, No. 3 (1975), p. 451.

**7** D. Bloxham, D, *The Great Game of Genocide: Imperialism, Nationalism and the Destruction of the Ottoman Armenians* (Oxford, 2005), p. 39.

**8** T. de Waal, *Great Catastrophe: Armenians and Turks in the Shadow of Genocide* (Oxford, 2015), p. 25.

**9** R. Hovannisian, 'The Armenian Genocide: Wartime Radicalization or Premeditated Continuum', in R. Hovannisian (ed.), *The Armenian Genocide: Cultural and Ethical Legacies* (New Brunswick, NJ and London, 2007), p. 6.

**10** Ibid., p. 7.

**11** U. Üngör, 'Seeing like a Nation-State: Young Turk Social Engineering in Eastern Turkey, 1913–1950', *Journal of Genocide Research* Vol. 10, No. 1 (2008), pp. 15–39.

**12** P. Balakian, *The Burning Tigris: The Armenian Genocide and America's Response* (New York, 2003), p. 164.

**13** Cited in R. Gellately and B. Kiernan, *The Specter of Genocide: Mass Murder in Historical Perspective* (Cambridge, 2003), p. 34.

**14** R. Suny, 'Empire and Nation: Armenians, Turks, and the End of the Ottoman Empire', *Armenian Forum* Vol. 1, No. 2 (1998), p. 46.

**15** On this, see T. Akçam, 'The Young Turks and the Plans for the Ethnic Homogenization of Anatolia', in O. Bartov and E. Weitz (eds), *Shatterzone of Empires: Coexistence and Violence in the German, Habsburg, Russian, and Ottoman Borderlands* (Bloomington, IN, 2013), pp. 258–80.

**16** Bloxham, 'The Armenian Genocide of 1915–1916', p. 154. On the conflict between the Ottoman and Russian Empires, see M. Reynolds, *Shattering Empires: The Clash and Collapse of the Ottoman and Russian Empires, 1908–1918* (Cambridge, 2011).

**17** On this, see Bloxham, 'The Armenian Genocide of 1915–1916', p. 188 and pp. 190–1. See also de Waal, *Great Catastrophe*, p. 31.

**18** J. Winter, 'Under Cover of War: The Armenian Genocide in the Context of Total War', in Gellately and Kiernan, *The Specter of Genocide*, p. 191.

**19** Bloxham, 'The Armenian Genocide of 1915–1916', p. 180.

**20** Ibid., p. 152.

**21** On this, see T. Akçam and U. Kurt, *The Spirit of the Laws: The Plunder of Wealth in the Armenian Genocide* (New York and Oxford, 2015).

**22** Bloxham, 'The Armenian Genocide of 1915–1916', p. 152.

**23** R. Adalian, 'The Armenian Genocide', in S. Totten and W. Parsons (eds), *Century of Genocide: Critical Essays and Eyewitness Accounts* (New York, 2009), p. 65.

**24** Bloxham, 'The Armenian Genocide of 1915–1916', p. 180.

**25** K. Derderian, 'Common Fate, Different Experience: Gender-specific Aspects of the Armenian Genocide, 1915–1917', *Holocaust and Genocide Studies* Vol. 19, No. 1 (2005), p. 2. On this, see also A. Holslag, 'Exposed Bodies: A Conceptual Approach to Sexual Violence during the Armenian Genocide', in A. Randall (ed.), *Genocide and Gender in the Twentieth Century: A Comparative Survey* (London, 2015), pp. 87–106.

**26** P. Balakian, 'Raphael Lemkin, Cultural Destruction, and the Armenian Genocide', *Holocaust and Genocide Studies* Vol. 27, No. 1 (2013), p. 63.

**27** Cited in A. Jones, *Genocide: A Comprehensive Introduction* (Oxford and New York, 2017), p. 211.

**28** For example, see K. Panian, *Goodbye, Antoura: A Memoir of the Armenian Genocide* (Stanford, CA, 2015); A. Marsoobian, *Fragments of a Lost Homeland: Remembering Armenia* (London, 2015).

**29** Cited in Adalian, 'The Armenian Genocide', in Totten and Parsons (eds), *Century of Genocide*, p. 86.

**30** M. Derderian, *Vergeen: A Survivor of the Armenian Genocide* (Los Angeles, CA, 1998), cited in Jones, *Genocide*, p. 110.

**31** See H. Travis, '"Native Christians Massacred": The Ottoman Genocide of the Assyrians during World War I', *Genocide Studies and Prevention* Vol. 1, No. 3 (2006), pp. 327–71. See also H. Travis, *Genocide in the Middle East: The Ottoman Empire, Iraq, and Sudan* (Durham, NC, 2010).

**32** On this, see D. Gaunt, *Massacres, Resistance, Protectors: Muslim-Christian Relations in Eastern Anatolia during World War I* (Piscataway, NJ, 2006).

**33** On this, see Jones, *Genocide*, pp. 225–9. See also T. Hofmann, M. Bjornlund and V. Meichanetsidis (eds), *The Genocide of the Ottoman Greeks: Studies on the State-Sponsored Campaign of Extermination of the Christians of Asia Minor (1912–1922) and its Aftermath: History, Law, Memory* (New York, 2011).

**34** Dadrian, *Warrant for Genocide*, p. 166.

**35** Ibid., p. 168.

**36** Hovannisian, 'The Armenian Genocide', p. 7.

# 3: The Nazi Genocide of the Jews

**1** D. Michman, 'The Jewish Dimension of the Holocaust in Dire Straits? Current Challenges of Interpretation and Scope', in N. Goda (ed.), *Jewish Histories of the Holocaust: New Transnational Approaches* (Oxford, 2014), p. 24.

2    A. Confino, *A World Without Jews: The Nazi Imagination from Persecution to Genocide* (New Haven, CT and London, 2014), p. 9.

3    E. Kurlander, *Hitler's Monsters: A Supernatural History of the Third Reich* (New Haven, CT and London, 2017), p. xvii.

4    I. Kershaw, *The Nazi Dictatorship: Problems and Perspectives of Interpretation* (London, 2015), pp. 109–55.

5    G. Fleming, *Hitler and the Final Solution* (Oxford, 1986).

6    L. Dawidowicz, *The War against the Jews, 1933–1945* (New York, 1975).

7    K. Schleunes, *The Twisted Road to Auschwitz: Nazi Policy toward the Jews, 1933–1939* (Urbana, IL, 1970).

8    D. Cesarani, *Final Solution: The Fate of the Jews 1933–49* (London, 2016), pp. xxix–xxx.

9    Kershaw, *The Nazi Dictatorship*.

10    C. Tatz, 'Genocide Studies: An Australian Perspective', *Genocide Studies and Prevention* Vol. 6, No. 3 (2011), p. 232.

11    Z. Bauman, *Modernity and the Holocaust* (Oxford, 1989).

12    D. Goldhagen, *Hitler's Willing Executioners* (New York, 1996).

13    On this, see G. Aly, *Hitler's Beneficiaries: Plunder, Racial War and the Nazi Welfare State* (New York, 2008).

14    E. Rentschler, 'The Legacy of Nazi Cinema: *Triumph of the Will* and *Jew Süss* Revisited', in J. Huener and F. Nicosia (eds), *The Arts in Nazi Germany: Continuity, Conformity, Change* (Oxford and New York, 2006), p. 72.

15    Ibid., p. 74.

16    Cesarani, *Final Solution*, p. 274.

17    W. Benz, *The Holocaust: A Short History* (London, 2000), p. 60.

18    On this, see C. Gerlach, 'The Wannsee Conference, the Fate of European Jews, and Hitler's Decision in Principle to Exterminate all European Jews', *Journal of Modern History* Vol. 70, No. 4 (1998), pp. 759–812.

19    M. Roseman, *The Villa, the Lake, the Meeting: Wannsee and the Final Solution* (London, 2003), pp. 87–8.

20    Cesarani, *Final Solution*, p. 795.

21    Michman, 'The Jewish Dimension of the Holocaust in Dire Straits? Current Challenges of Interpretation and Scope', pp. 25–6.

**22** Cesarani, *Final Solution*, p. 795.

**23** For a useful summary of this, see W. Benz, *The Holocaust: A Short History* (London, 2000), pp. 131–56.

**24** L. Bitton-Jackson, *I Have Lived a Thousand Years: Growing up in the Holocaust* (London, 1999), p. 77.

**25** E. Wiesel, *Night* (London, 2006), p. 37.

**26** S. Venezia, *Inside the Gas Chambers: Eight Months in the Sonderkommando of Auschwitz* (Cambridge, 2009), pp. 64–5.

**27** On this, see Cesarani, *Final Solution*, pp. 762 and 765–6.

**28** Ibid., p. 796.

**29** Michman, 'The Jewish Dimension of the Holocaust in Dire Straits? Current Challenges of Interpretation and Scope', p. 25.

# 4: The Nazi Genocide of the Sinti and Roma

**1** I. Hancock, 'Romanies and the Holocaust', in D. Stone (ed.), *The Historiography of the Holocaust* (Basingstoke, 2004), p. 393.

**2** D. Kenrick and G. Puxon, *The Destiny of Europe's Gypsies* (London, 1972).

**3** Examples of these publications include: O. Rosenberg, *A Gypsy in Auschwitz* (as told to Ulrich Herzenberger), translated by Helmut Bögler (London, 1999); T. Sonnemann, *Shared Sorrows: A Gypsy Family Remembers the Holocaust* (Hatfield, 2002); and W. Winter, *Winter Time: Memoirs of a German Sinto who Survived Auschwitz* (Hatfield, 2004).

**4** D. Kenrick and G. Puxon, *Gypsies under the Swastika* (Hatfield, 1995), p. 10. See also revised edition, D. Kenrick and G. Puxon, *Gypsies under the Swastika* (Hatfield, 2009).

**5** I. Hancock, *The Pariah Syndrome: An Account of Gypsy Slavery and Persecution* (Ann Arbor, MI, 1987), pp. 58–9.

**6** Cited in M. Burleigh and W. Wippermann, *The Racial State: Germany 1933–1945* (Cambridge, 1991), pp. 114–15.

**7** S. Milton, '"Gypsies" as Social Outsiders in Nazi Germany', in R. Gellately and N. Stoltzfus (eds), *Social Outsiders in Nazi Germany* (Princeton, NJ, 2001), p. 212.

**8** Milton, '"Gypsies" as Social Outsiders in Nazi Germany', p. 214.

**9** Cited in Milton, '"Gypsies" as Social Outsiders in Nazi Germany', p. 219.

**10** Cited in Burleigh and Wippermann, *The Racial State*, p. 120.

**11** Ibid., p. 121.

**12** K. Fings, H. Heuss and F. Sparing, *From 'Race Science' to the Camps: The Gypsies during the Second World War* (Hatfield, 1997), p. 55.

**13** Ibid., p. 40.

**14** Milton, '"Gypsies" as Social Outsiders in Nazi Germany', p. 220.

**15** Cited in B. Alt and S. Folts, *Weeping Violins: The Gypsy Tragedy In Europe* (Kirksville, MO, 1996), p. 25.

**16** Alt and Folts, *Weeping Violins*, p. 24.

**17** G. Lewy, 'Himmler and the "Racially Pure Gypsies"', *Journal of Contemporary History* Vol. 34, No. 2 (1999), p. 202.

**18** M. Zimmermann, 'From Discrimination to the "Family Camp" at Auschwitz', in W. Benz and B. Distel (eds), *Dachau Review 2. History of Nazi Concentration Camps: Studies, Reports, Documents* (Dachau, 1990), p. 98.

**19** Cited in Alt and Folts, *Weeping Violins*, p. 1.

**20** Cited in Lewy, *The Nazi Persecution of the Gypsies*, p. 77.

**21** On this, see relevant chapters in A. Weiss-Wendt and R. Yeomans (eds), *Racial Science in Hitler's New Europe, 1938–1945* (Lincoln, NE, 2013).

**22** Cited in Lewy, 'Himmler and the "Racially Pure Gypsies"', p. 205.

**23** Lewy, 'Himmler and the "Racially Pure Gypsies"', p. 214.

**24** Zimmermann, 'From Discrimination to the "Family Camp" at Auschwitz', p. 106.

**25** Ibid., p. 108.

**26** Cited in Fings, *From 'Race Science' to the Camps*, p. 96.

**27** Cited in Alt and Folts, *Weeping Violins*, p. 55.

**28** Cited in Fings, *From 'Race Science' to the Camps*, pp. 108–9.

**29** Zimmermann, 'From Discrimination to the "Family Camp" at Auschwitz', pp. 109–10.

**30** Cited in Alt and Folts, *Weeping Violins*, p. 49.

**31** Alt and Folts, *Weeping Violins*, p. 52.

**32** Cited in Lewy, *The Nazi Persecution of the Gypsies*, p. 174.

**33** Cited in Hancock, 'Romanies and the Holocaust', p. 391.

## 5: Cambodia: Genocide or Politicide?

1   M. Midlarsky, *The Killing Trap: Genocide in the Twentieth Century* (Cambridge, 2005), p. 309.

2   Ibid., p. 310.

3   F. Dikötter, *Mao's Great Famine* (London, 2011), p. xii.

4   A. Jones, *Genocide: A Comprehensive Introduction* (London and New York, 2017), p. 399.

5   R. Conquest, *The Harvest of Sorrow: Soviet Collectivisation and the Terror-Famine* (Oxford, 1986), p. 306.

6   Midlarsky, *The Killing Trap*, p. 324.

7   See D. Chandler, *The Tragedy of Cambodian History: Politics, War and Revolution since 1945* (New Haven, CT and London, 1991) and D. Chandler, *Brother Number One: A Political Biography of Pol Pot* (Boulder, CO, 1999).

8   Chandler, *The Tragedy of Cambodian History*, p. 285.

9   M. Vickery, *Cambodia 1975–1982* (Boston, MA, 1984), p. 7.

10  Chandler, *The Tragedy of Cambodian History*, pp. 289–90.

11  Ibid., p. 287.

12  S. Thion, 'The Cambodian Idea of Revolution', in D. Chandler and B. Kiernan (eds), *Revolution and its Aftermath: Eight Essays* (New Haven, CT, 1983), p. 28.

13  B. Kiernan, *The Pol Pot Regime: Race, Power, and Genocide in Cambodia under the Khmer Rouge, 1975–1979* (New Haven, CT, 1996), pp. 26–7.

14  A. Barnett, 'Democratic Kampuchea: A Highly Centralized Dictatorship', in Chandler and Kiernan (eds), *Revolution and its Aftermath*, p. 212.

15  Cited in K. Jackson, *Cambodia 1975–1978: Rendezvous with Death* (Princeton, NJ, 1989), p. 185.

16  Cited in ibid., p. 182.

17  B. Valentino, *Final Solutions: Mass Killing and Genocide in the Twentieth Century* (Ithaca, NY, 2005), p. 143.

18  B. Kiernan, 'The Cambodian Genocide, 1975–1979', in S. Totten and W. Parsons (eds), *Century of Genocide: Critical Essays and Eyewitness Accounts* (Abingdon and New York, 2009), p. 346.

19  C. Boua, 'Genocide of a Religious Group: Pol Pot and Cambodia's Buddhist Monks', in P. Bushnell, V. Shlapentokh, C. Vanderpool and J. Sundram (eds), *State-Organized Terror: The Case of Violent Internal Repression* (Boulder, CO, 1991), p. 227.

**20**  B. Kiernan, 'The Cambodian Genocide, 1975–1979', p. 347.

**21**  Ibid., p. 348.

**22**  Ibid.

**23**  Chandler, *Brother Number One*, p. 129.

**24**  Cited in J. Waller, *Becoming Evil: How Ordinary People Commit Genocide and Mass Killing* (Oxford, 2007), pp. 164–7.

**25**  E. Weitz, *A Century of Genocide: Utopias of Race and Nation* (Princeton, NJ, 2003), p. 179.

**26**  Ibid., p. 153.

**27**  On this, see D. Chandler, *Voices from S–21: Terror and History in Pol Pot's Secret Prison* (Berkeley and Los Angeles, CA, 1999).

**28**  Midlarsky, *The Killing Trap*, p. 314.

**29**  A. Hinton, *Why Did They Kill? Cambodia in the Shadow of Genocide* (Berkeley, CA, 2005), p. 25.

**30**  Kiernan, 'The Cambodian Genocide, 1975–1979', in Totten and Parsons (eds), *Century of Genocide*, p. 360.

**31**  S. Ratner and J. Abrams, *Accountability for Human Rights Atrocities in International Law: Beyond the Nuremberg Legacy* (Oxford, 1997), p. 244.

# 6: Genocide in the Former Yugoslavia

**1**  See R. Kaplan, *Balkan Ghosts: A Journey Through History* (New York, 2005) and M. Biondich, *The Balkans: Revolution, War, and Political Violence since 1878* (Oxford, 2011).

**2**  N. Cigar, *Genocide in Bosnia: The Policy of 'Ethnic Cleansing'* (College Station, TX, 1995).

**3**  S. Woodward, *Balkan Tragedy: Chaos and Dissolution after the Cold War* (Washington, DC, 1995), p. 267.

**4**  M. Midlarsky, *The Killing Trap: Genocide in the Twentieth Century* (Cambridge, 2005), p. 130.

**5**  W. Schabas, 'Was Genocide Committed in Bosnia and Herzegovina? First Judgments of the International Criminal Tribunal for the Former Yugoslavia', *Fordham International Law Journal* Vol. 25, No. 1 (2001), pp. 23–53 and W. Schabas, 'Problems of International Codification – Were the Atrocities in Cambodia and Kosovo Genocide?', *New England Law Review* Vol. 35, No. 2 (2001), pp. 287–302.

**6**  On this, see T. Dulić, *Utopias of Nation: Local Mass Killings in Bosnia and Herzegovina, 1941–42* (Uppsala, 2005); K. Pavlowitch,

*Hitler's New Disorder: The Second World War in Yugoslavia* (London, 2008); P. Mojzes, *Balkan Genocides: Holocaust and Ethnic Cleansing in the Twentieth Century* (Lanham, MD, 2011), pp. 45–108; and B. Shepherd, *Terror in the Balkans: German Armies and Partisan Warfare* (Cambridge, MA, 2012).

7    On this, see R. Hayden, 'Mass Killings and Images of Genocide in Bosnia, 1941–5 and 1992–5', in D. Stone (ed.), *The Historiography of Genocide* (Basingstoke, 2010), pp. 487–516.

8    G. Toal and C. Dahlman, *Bosnia Remade: Ethnic Cleansing and its Reversal* (Oxford, 2011), p. 18.

9    M. Mennecke, 'Genocidal Violence in the Former Yugoslavia', in S. Totten and W. Parsons (eds), *Century of Genocide* (Abingdon and New York, 2009), p. 509.

10   On Karadžić, see R. Donia, *Radovan Karadžić: Architect of the Bosnian Genocide* (Cambridge, 2015).

11   A. Jones, *Genocide: A Comprehensive Introduction* (Oxford and New York, 2017), p. 435.

12   On this, see H. Brunborg, T. Lyngstad and H. Urdal, 'Accounting for Genocide: How Many Were Killed in Srebrenica?', *European Journal of Population* Vol. 19 (2003), pp. 229–48. On Srebrenica, see also D. Rohde, *Endgame: The Betrayal and Fall of Srebrenica. Europe's Worst Massacre since World War II* (New York, 1997) and S. Leydesdorff, *Surviving the Bosnian Genocide: The Women of Srebrenica Speak* (Bloomington, IN, 2011).

13   Cited in J. Honig and N. Both, *Srebrenica: Record of a War Crime* (New York, 1996), p. 56.

14   J. Semelin, 'Analysis of a Mass Crime: Ethnic Cleansing in the Former Yugoslavia, 1991–1999', in R. Gellately and B. Kiernan (eds), *The Specter of Genocide: Mass Murder in Historical Perspective* (Cambridge, 2003), p. 365.

15   Cited in ibid., p. 366.

16   See A. Stiglmayer (ed.), *Mass Rape: The War against Women in Bosnia-Herzegovina* (Lincoln, NE, 1994); B. Allen, *Rape Warfare: The Hidden Genocide in Bosnia-Herzegovina and Croatia* (St. Paul, MN, 1996); C. Rittner and J. Roth (eds), *Rape: Weapon of War and Genocide* (St. Paul, MN, 2012); and P. Weitsman, 'Constructions of Identity and Sexual Violence in Wartime: The Case of Bosnia', in A. Randall (ed.), *Genocide and Gender in the Twentieth Century: A Comparative Survey* (London, 2015), pp. 121–39.

17   On this, see E. Tabeau and J. Bijak, 'War-related Deaths in the 1992–1995 Armed Conflicts in Bosnia and Herzegovina: A Critique

of Previous Estimates and Recent Results', *European Journal of Population* Vol. 21 (2005), pp. 187–215.

**18**   On this, see Mojzes, *Balkan Genocides*, pp. 197–219; T. Judah, *Kosovo: War and Revenge* (New Haven, CT, 2002) and T. Judah, *Kosovo: What Everyone Needs to Know* (Oxford, 2008).

**19**   J. Byford, 'Remembering Jasenovac: Survivor Testimonies and the Cultural Dimension of Bearing Witness', *Holocaust and Genocide Studies* Vol. 28, No. 1 (2014), p. 62.

# 7: Genocide in Rwanda

**1**   R. Lemarchand, 'The 1994 Rwanda Genocide', in S. Totten and W. Parsons (eds), *Century of Genocide: Critical Essays and Eyewitness Accounts* (Abingdon and New York, 2009), p. 484.

**2**   G. Prunier, *The Rwanda Crisis: History of a Genocide* (New York, 1995), p. 39.

**3**   S. Straus, 'The Historiography of the Rwandan Genocide', in D. Stone (ed.), *The Historiography of Genocide* (Basingstoke, 2010), p. 518.

**4**   Lemarchand, 'The 1994 Rwanda Genocide', p. 485.

**5**   Straus, 'The Historiography of the Rwandan Genocide', p. 520.

**6**   R. Lemarchand, *The Dynamics of Violence in Central Africa* (Philadelphia, PA, 2009), p. 92.

**7**   On the role of the radio, see F. Chalk, 'Hate Radio in Rwanda', in H. Adelman and A. Suhrke (eds), *The Path of a Genocide: The Rwanda Crisis from Uganda to Zaire* (New Brunswick, NJ, 1999), pp. 93–107 and D. Li, 'Echoes of Violence: Considerations on Radio and Genocide in Rwanda', *Journal of Genocide Research* Vol. 6, No. 1 (2004), pp. 9–27.

**8**   R. Melson, 'Modern Genocide in Rwanda: Ideology, Revolution, War, and Mass Murder in an African State', in R. Gellately and B. Kiernan, *The Specter of Genocide: Mass Murder in Historical Perspective* (Cambridge, 2003), p. 334.

**9**   C. Scherrer, *Genocide and Crisis in Central Africa: Conflict Roots, Mass Violence and Regional War* (Westport, CT, 2002), p. 109.

**10**   Lemarchand, *The Dynamics of Violence in Central Africa*, p. 92.

**11**   Prunier, *The Rwanda Crisis*, p. 232.

**12**   On female perpetrators, see N. Hogg and M. Drumbl, 'Women as Perpetrators: Agency and Authority in Genocidal Rwanda', in A. Randall (ed.), *Genocide and Gender in the Twentieth Century*

(London, 2015), pp. 189–211. On estimated perpetrator numbers, see S. Straus, 'How Many Perpetrators Were There in the Rwandan Genocide? An Estimate', *Journal of Genocide Research* Vol. 6, No. 1 (2004), pp. 85–98.

**13** M. Mamdani, *When Victims Become Killers: Colonialism, Nativism, and the Genocide in Rwanda* (Princeton, NJ, 2001), p. 225.

**14** Cited in J. Hatzfeld, *Life Laid Bare: The Survivors in Rwanda Speak* (New York, 2007), p. 73.

**15** A. Jones, *Genocide: A Comprehensive Introduction* (Oxford and New York, 2017), p. 484.

**16** Ibid., p. 485.

**17** Cited in Hatzfeld, *Life Laid Bare*, p. 131. For more eyewitness accounts, see S. Totten and R. Ubaldo (eds), *We Cannot Forget: Interviews with Survivors of the 1994 Genocide in Rwanda* (New Brunswick, NJ and London, 2011).

**18** See R. Dallaire, *Shake Hands with the Devil: The Failure of Humanity in Rwanda* (New York, 2004).

**19** Straus, 'The Historiography of the Rwandan Genocide', p. 522.

# 8: Genocide in Sudan

**1** M. Daly, *Darfur's Sorrow: The Forgotten History of a Humanitarian Disaster* (Cambridge, 2010), p. 281.

**2** M. Mamdani, 'The Politics of Naming: Genocide, Civil War, Insurgency', in S. Hassan and C. Ray (eds), *Darfur and the Crisis of Governance in Sudan: A Critical Reader* (Ithaca, NY, 2009), p. 145.

**3** Daly, *Darfur's Sorrow*, p. 293.

**4** C. Gallo, 'Researching Genocide in Africa: Establishing Ethnological and Historical Context', in A. Jones (ed.), *New Directions in Genocide Research* (London and New York, 2012), p. 231.

**5** Ibid., pp. 237–8.

**6** On this, see R. O'Fahey, *The Dar Fur Sultanate* (London, 2007).

**7** R. Collins, 'Disaster in Darfur: Historical Overview', in S. Totten and E. Markussen (eds), *Genocide in Darfur: Investigating the Atrocities in the Sudan* (New York and London, 2006), p. 6. This term is also used and explained in G. Prunier, *Darfur: A 21st Century Genocide* (Ithaca, NY, 2008).

**8** Gallo, 'Researching Genocide in Africa', p. 242.

**9** Collins, 'Disaster in Darfur: Historical Overview', p. 6.

**10**  Gallo, 'Researching Genocide in Africa', p. 245.

**11**  Daly, *Darfur's Sorrow*, p. 278.

**12**  A. de Waal, 'Darfur and the Failure of the Responsibility to Protect', *International Affairs* Vol. 83, No. 6 (2007), p. 1040.

**13**  Collins, 'Disaster in Darfur: Historical Overview', p. 10.

**14**  Ibid., p. 10.

**15**  Daly, *Darfur's Sorrow*, p. 281.

**16**  Ibid., p. 282.

**17**  Ibid., p. 283.

**18**  Ibid., p. 283.

**19**  Collins, 'Disaster in Darfur: Historical Overview', p. 12.

**20**  Daly, *Darfur's Sorrow*, pp. 282–3.

**21**  Cited in S. Tottten and W. Parsons (eds), *Century of Genocide: Critical Essays and Eyewitness Accounts* (New York and London, 2009), pp. 593–6.

**22**  Cited in ibid., pp. 597–8.

**23**  Collins, 'Disaster in Darfur: Historical Overview', p. 14.

**24**  Cited in ibid., p. 14.

**25**  Ibid., p. 15.

**26**  Daly, *Darfur's Sorrow*, p. 285.

**27**  On 'embattled humanitarianism', see Prunier, *Darfur: A 21st Century Genocide*.

**28**  Daly, *Darfur's Sorrow*, p. 294.

**29**  Collins, 'Disaster in Darfur: Historical Overview', p. 21.

**30**  Cited in Daly, *Darfur's Sorrow*, p. 291. See also, M. Kapila, *Against a Tide of Evil: How One Man Became the Whistleblower to the First Mass Murder of the Twenty-First Century* (Edinburgh and London, 2013).

**31**  Prunier, *Darfur: A 21st Century Genocide*.

**32**  On the *Janjaweed*, see A. Haggar, 'The Origins and Organization of the Janjaweed in Darfur', in A. de Waal, *War in Darfur and the Search for Peace* (Cambridge, MA, 2007), pp. 113–39.

**33**  S. Totten and E. Markussen (eds), *Genocide in Darfur: Investigating the Atrocities in the Sudan* (New York and London, 2006), p. xiv.

**34**  de Waal, 'Darfur and the Failure of the Responsibility to Protect', p. 1043.

**35**  M. Mamdani, *Saviors and Survivors: Darfur, Politics and the War on Terror* (London, 2009), p. 279.

**36**  Daly, *Darfur's Sorrow*, p. 269.

**37**  Ibid., p. 272.

**38**  Prunier, *Darfur: A 21st Century Genocide*.

**39**  de Waal, 'Darfur and the Failure of the Responsibility to Protect',
p. 1041.

## 9: Themes

**1**  A. Randall (ed.), *Genocide and Gender in the Twentieth Century*
(London, 2015), p. 2.

**2**  A. Jones, 'Problems of Gendercide', in A. Jones (ed.), *Gendercide
and Genocide* (Nashville, TN, 2004), p. 264.

**3**  Important works include: M. A. Warren, *Gendercide: The
Implications of Sex Selection* (Totowa, NJ, 1985); H. Fein,
'Genocide and Gender: The Uses of Woman and Group Destiny',
*Journal of Genocide Research* Vol. 1, No. 1 (1999), pp. 43–63;
Jones, (ed.), *Gendercide and Genocide*; R. Smith, 'Women and
Genocide: Notes on an Unwritten History', *Holocaust and Genocide
Studies* Vol. 8, No. 3 (1994), pp. 315–34; Randall (ed.), *Genocide and
Gender in the Twentieth Century*.

**4**  E. von Joeden-Forgey, 'Genocidal Masculinity', in A. Jones (ed.),
*New Directions in Genocide Research* (London and New York,
2012), pp. 77–8.

**5**  Ibid., p. 78.

**6**  J. Nagel, 'Masculinity and Nationalism: Gender and Sexuality in the
Making of Nations', *Ethnic and Racial Studies* Vol. 21, No. 2 (1998),
p. 243.

**7**  Joeden-Forgey, 'Genocidal Masculinity', p. 80.

**8**  Ibid., p. 83.

**9**  Ibid., p. 92.

**10**  P. Drumond, 'Invisible Males: A Critical Assessment of UN Gender
Mainstreaming Policies in the Congolese Genocide', in Jones (ed.),
*New Directions in Genocide Research*, p. 98.

**11**  P. Drumond, 'Invisible Males', p 106.

**12**  On this, see A. Stiglmayer (ed.), *Mass Rape: The War against
Women in Bosnia-Herzegovina* (Lincoln, NE, 1994); B. Allen, *Rape
Warfare: The Hidden Genocide in Bosnia-Herzegovina and Croatia*
(St. Paul, MN, 1996); C. Rittner and J. Roth (eds), *Rape: Weapon
of War and Genocide* (St. Paul, MN, 2012); and P. Weitsman,

'Constructions of Identity and Sexual Violence in Wartime: The Case of Bosnia', in Randall (ed.), *Genocide and Gender in the Twentieth Century*, pp. 121–39. See also S. Leydesdorff, *Surviving the Bosnian Genocide: The Women of Srebrenica Speak* (Bloomington, IN, 2015).

**13** Randall (ed.), *Genocide and Gender in the Twentieth Century*, p. 4.

**14** On this, see R. Jackson, *Sovereignty: The Evolution of an Idea* (London, 2007). On issues of intervention, see also, N. Mills and K. Brunner (eds), *The New Killing Fields: Massacre and the Politics of Intervention* (New York, 2002).

**15** On this, see P. Bartrop, 'Political Realism, Sovereignty and Intervention: Is Genocide Prevention Really Possible in a World of Nation States?', in D. Mayersen and A. Pohlman (eds), *Genocide and Mass Atrocities in Asia: Legacies and Prevention* (London, 2014), pp. 119–35.

**16** On this, see D. Bosco, *Rough Justice: The International Criminal Court in a World of Power Politics* (New York and Oxford, 2014) and W. Schabas, *An Introduction to the International Criminal Court* (Cambridge, 2011).

**17** A. de Waal, 'Darfur and the Failure of the Responsibility to Protect', *International Affairs* Vol. 83, No. 6 (2007), p. 1045. See also V. Holt and T. Berkman, *The Impossible Mandate: Military Preparedness, the Responsibility to Protect and Modern Peace Operations* (Washington, DC, 2006).

**18** S. Straus, *Fundamentals of Genocide and Mass Atrocity Prevention* (Washington, DC, 2016), p. 283.

**19** Ibid., p. 401.

**20** A. Bellamy and T. Dunne, 'R2P in Theory and Practice', in A. Bellamy and T. Dunne, *The Oxford Handbook of the Responsibility to Protect* (Oxford, 2016), p. 11.

**21** Straus, *Fundamentals of Genocide and Mass Atrocity Prevention*, p. 365.

**22** A. LeBor, *'Complicity with Evil': The United Nations in the Age of Genocide* (New Haven, CT and London, 2006), p. xiv.

**23** C. Rittner, J. Roth and J. Smith (eds), *Will Genocide Ever End?* (St. Paul, MN, 2002), p. 205.

**24** M. Ignatieff, 'Intervention and State Failure', in Mills and Brunner (eds), *The New Killing Fields*, p. 242.

**25** On this, see D. Scheffer, 'Genocide and Atrocity Crimes', *Genocide Studies and Prevention* Vol. 1, No. 3 (2007), pp. 229–50. See also M. Mennecke, 'What's in a Name? Reflections on Using, Not Using and Overusing the "G Word"', *Genocide Studies and Prevention* Vol. 2, No. 1 (2007), pp. 57–72.

26  M. Mamdani, *Saviors and Survivors: Darfur, Politics and the War on Terror* (London, 2009), p. 300.

27  On this, see A. Hinton (ed.), *Transitional Justice: Global Mechanisms and Local Realities after Genocide and Mass Violence* (New Brunswick, NJ and London, 2010).

28  A. Williams, *A Passing Fury: Searching for Justice at the End of World War II* (London, 2016), p. 432.

29  On this, see H. Ball, *Prosecuting War Crimes and Genocide: The Twentieth Century Experience* (Lawrence, KS, 1999); N. Ehrenfreund, *The Nuremberg Legacy: How the Nazi War Crimes Trials Changed the Course of History* (New York, 2007); and K. Priemal and A. Stiller (eds), *Reassessing the Nuremberg Military Tribunals: Transitional Justice, Trial Narratives, and Historiography* (New York, 2012).

30  On this, see R. Kolb, *The International Court of Justice* (Oxford, 2013); and C. Tams and J. Sloan (eds), *The Development of International Law by the International Court of Justice* (Oxford, 2013).

31  On this, see L. Fletcher and H. Weinstein, 'A World unto Itself? The Application of International Justice in the Former Yugoslavia', in E. Stover and H. Weinstein (eds), *My Neighbor, My Enemy: Justice and Community in the Aftermath of Mass Atrocity* (Cambridge, 2004), pp. 29–48.

32  On this, see W. Schabas, *The UN International Criminal Tribunals: The Former Yugoslavia, Rwanda and Sierra Leone* (Cambridge, 2006).

33  On this, see J. Armatta, *Twilight of Impunity: The War Crimes Trial of Slobodan Milošević* (Durham, NC, 2010) and T. Waters (ed.), *The Milošević Trial: An Autopsy* (Oxford, 2014).

34  On this, see A. des Forges and T. Longman, 'Legal Responses to Genocide in Rwanda', in Stover and Weinstein (eds), *My Neighbor, My Enemy*, pp. 49–68.

35  On this, see T. Cruvellier, *Court of Remorse: Inside the International Criminal Tribunal for Rwanda* (Madison, WI, 2010).

36  U. Karakezi, A. Nshimiyamana and B. Mutamba, 'Localizing Justice: Gacaca Courts in Post-genocide Rwanda', in Stover and Weinstein (eds), *My Neighbor, My Enemy*, p. 69. On this, see also J. Melvin, *Reconciling Rwanda: Unity, Nationality and State Control* (London, 2015), pp. 75–95.

37  On these, see C. Surabhi, 'The International Crimes Tribunal in Bangladesh: Silencing Fair Comment', *Journal of Genocide*

*Research* Vol. 17, No. 2 (2015), pp. 211–20; and E. Oglesby and D. Nelson, 'Guatemala's Genocide Trial and the Nexus of Racism and Counterinsurgency', *Journal of Genocide Research* Vol. 18, Nos. 2–3 (2016), pp. 133–42.

**38** On this, see Schabas, *An Introduction to the International Criminal Court.*

**39** D. MacDonald, *Identity Politics in the Age of Genocide: The Holocaust and Historical Representation* (London and New York, 2008), p. 195.

**40** On representations of genocide, see J. Michalczyk and R. Herlmick (eds), *Through a Darkly Lens: Films of Genocide, Ethnic Cleansing, and Atrocities* (New York, 2013); S. Gigliotti, J. Colomb and C. Gould (eds), *Ethics, Art, and Representation of the Holocaust* (Lanham, MD, 2014); and R. Jinks, *Representing Genocide: The Holocaust as Paradigm* (London, 2016).

**41** A. Confino, 'Collective Memory and Cultural History: Problems of Method', *American Historical Review* Vol. 107 (1997), p. 1390.

**42** D. Stone, 'Memory, Memorials and Museums', in D. Stone (ed.), *The Historiography of the Holocaust* (Basingstoke, 2004), p. 508.

**43** Ibid., p. 510.

**44** J. Young, *At Memory's Edge: After-Images of the Holocaust in Contemporary Art and Architecture* (New Haven, CT, 2000), p. 198.

**45** On this, see Stone, 'Memory, Memorials and Museums', p. 512.

**46** Young, *At Memory's Edge*, p. 7.

**47** Stone, 'Memory, Memorials and Museums', p. 514.

**48** Young, *At Memory's Edge*, p. 7.

**49** Stone, 'Memory, Memorials and Museums', p. 525.

**50** See C. Sharples and O. Jensen (eds), *Britain and the Holocaust: Remembering and Representing War and Genocide* (Basingstoke, 2013); and P. Novick, *The Holocaust and Collective Memory: The American Experience* (London, 2001).

**51** A. Huyssen, *Twilight Memories: Marking Time in a Culture of Amnesia* (New York, 1995), p. 518.

**52** See A. Pearce, 'Britain's Holocaust Memorial Day: Inculcating "British" or "European" Holocaust Consciousness?', in Sharples and Jensen (eds), *Britain and the Holocaust*, pp. 190–211.

**53** On this, see J. Ledgerwood, 'The Cambodian Tuol Sleng Museum of Genocidal Crimes', in D. Lorey and W. Beezley, *Genocide, Collective Violence, and Popular Memory: The Politics of*

*Remembrance in the Twentieth Century*, pp. 103–22.

**54**   R. Hughes, 'Memory and Sovereignty in Post–1979 Cambodia: Choeung Ek and Local Genocide Memorials', in S. Cook (ed.), *Genocide in Cambodia and Rwanda: New Perspectives* (Piscataway, NJ, 2005), pp. 269–92.

**55**   Ibid., p. 286.

**56**   J. Tyner, *Landscape, Memory, and Post-Violence in Cambodia* (London and New York, 2017).

# Conclusion

**1**   P. Levi, *If This is a Man* (London, 2000), p. 58.

**2**   L. Bitton-Jackson, *I Have Lived a Thousand Years: Growing Up in the Holocaust* (London, 1999), p. 9.

# Index

Page numbers in *italics* refer to figures and maps.